Stones
Winds
and Life

A Collection of Poems, Plays, Short Stories, and Tales
by David Sweet

Illustrations by Rick Farrell

www.sweetpoetry.com

DAVID SWEET, INC.

Stones
Winds
and Life

THE WORK IN THIS BOOK IS DEDICATED TO SOMEBODY

Book Design: Robert Brünz
Text Editing: Val Dumond
Hand Lettering: Ruth McDonald-Gates
Author's Bio: Kristin Tomlinson

Published by DAVID SWEET, INC.
Tacoma, Washington, United States of America

Copyright © 2000 David W. Sweet

First Edition

All rights reserved. This publication contains the original work of the author, published here for the first time. All work is protected under the copyright and no part of this publication may be reproduced, stored in a retrieval system, or transmitted in any form or by any means, electronic, mechanical, photocopying, recording, or otherwise, without prior consent of the author.

ISBN #0-615-11779-1

Printed in the United States of America

Contents

STONES
1

STARTING
4

THOUGHT FORMS
7

CLUES
8

LIFE IS ON TIME
11

DIRTY FEAST
12

PERSONAL
15

IN THE MOMENT
18

DIMENSIONS
19

HUMILIATION
21

A HOLE IN MY SOUL
23

YOU CAN'T HIDE
24

TAPS
27

LAST CALL
30

GOOD
31

TOM
32

OMEN — 30°
39

SHADOWS OF DECEPTION
41

THE OTHER SIDE
42

OUTLAW'S END
43

THE LOST SOULS
44

Stones
Winds
and Life

MASKS
46

FORTUNES
48

THE HORSEMAN
49

THE AWAKENING
50

ECHOES TO REMEMBER
53

SEEDS
55

ABILENE
58

GENERALS AND PAWNS
61

NO END
62

FIELD OF "HONOR"
63

CAISSONS OF THOUGHT
65

TWELVE
66

AN OFFER TO HELP
71

ANGELS' KEEP
75

CLOSED
76

MISSILES
79

NO TITLE
80

BILLBOARDS
81

CAFFEINE POLKA
82

BADLANDS BOB
85

LET THE CHILDREN BE
90

ANGELS' HELP
92

HOLOCAUST
95

EGO WORLD (A PLAY)
98

ELECTRIC PARENTS
101

WELCOME BACK TO EGO WORLD!
102

COLLECTING
108

TEXAS TWILIGHT
111

THE SEA
113

WINTER
114

FORESTS
117

PLEASE
118

WHITE NOISE
120

GREAT APPLAUSE
122

THE KINGDOM
125

THANK YOU ALL
133

BATTLE FATIGUE
134

JOURNEYS
136

DRAGON'S HELP
141

PASSING
146

WINDS
149

FALL THOUGHTS
157

VICTORY
159

LOST
162

Stones
Winds
and Life

STONES

The old man paused to rest by the street. He had taken this trip each day up the hill from the market place to his cottage on the crest of the hill. Today was different, however. His spirit was burdened.

As he reflected out on the view of the sea, he heard a voice, "Your footsteps are very heavy today."

He looked around.

"I *said* your footsteps are very heavy today."

Again he looked around. Right, left, to the archway of the building behind him. He saw no one close.

"I said your footsteps are heavier today than usual."

Now with that the man leaped to his feet and looked all around. No one in the windows above, no one near. "This is not a day for jokes or trickery," he explained, still looking around.

"I know, your footsteps tell me that," was the answer.

"Where are you? Who are you?" asked the old man.

"You're standing on me," was the reply.

"Very funny," spoke the old man.

"No really, you are. I'm part of the Earth. I am the spirit of these granite cobblestones. I'm still of the Earth, you see, just moved from my original location. My powers are still very much intact, however."

"Why are you speaking with me?" asked the old one.

"Because you are very burdened today, your feet are heavy like stone, your spirit is but a flicker," was the reply.

"That is true. It is a sad day," the old man said.

"It's about the children or young ones, isn't it?"

"Yes, you are right. Many more are joining the legions and going off to war," said the old man.

"And they won't all be coming back, will they?" was the reply.

"No, they won't. And those who do will most likely be crippled in body or crippled in the mind," said the old man.

"Yes, I can feel the difference in walk and the spirit of those affected," said the stone, "and of course there is a complete absence of many, like today. Their echo is enormous, a large void to fill, indeed."

"Why do you share this with me?" asked the old man.

"Because the Earth wants you to know that your burden and sorrow are shared, and felt as well. Sometimes even the sea or forest cannot soften or lighten these loads, so a more direct communication is needed. Instead of allowing my presence to work as a huge bit of stone in the mountains for escapes or retreats during walks, I have been moved to the streets. Rather effective, wouldn't you say?"

The old man was quiet. Then he spoke, "You've helped me before, haven't you?"

"Yes."

"When my wife died?"

"Yes, you noticed."

"Can I do anything to repay you?"

"When you walk on me, just notice, that is all."

"It's the feeling, isn't it?" replied the old man.

"Yes. Call it a solidness underfoot, assuredness, whatever. I know you can't describe it exactly, but what you're feeling is correct. You're simply never alone, either in times of great joy and celebration, or as today, in sorrow."

"Yes, I have felt this before," replied the old man, "but fleetingly, not as if it's something I could do always."

"Well, now you can," replied the stone.

The old man shook his head and looked around quickly. No one was there, not even close. Had he been dreaming? He laughed aloud and tears came to his eyes. As he resumed his journey up the hill, picking up his stride, he said simply, "Thank you."

"My pleasure, always," was the reply.

STARTING

Problems... problems...
I've got to go,
Whip things into shape,
Achieve the even flow.

Dissect and calculate.
Fit the curve.
Keep my life in line
Never to swerve.

Run the charts,
Run the graphs,
No land in sight.
Do I fit this raft?

Churn 'em and burn 'em.
Achieve a fearful pace.
I see my family
But not their face.

"Why is this?" I say.
"In order for pay
I must tax myself
To the limit each day?"

So I stopped to ponder
And walked the beach.
God said simply,
"It is all within reach."

To create with the hands,
To compose with the mind,
It is for you all.
For some it just takes time.

The secret is to watch,
Catch the hints when they are sent,
Seize the moments,
Make them well spent.

Solving just problems
Day after day
Turns your mind
Not unlike clay.

Look to create.
Take a simple thought.
Each time is different,
Like the flowing ink blot.

Clear the cobwebs,
Take a deep breath,
Pull your creativity
Back from death.

Choose to be silent,
Choose to be still.
In the charred forest
There can be a thrill.

It is God's intent
For you to invent.
"To the Grindstone," they say.
But, alas, look to the creative way.

Achieving balance
Is another term.
"Freeing up may at first
Make you squirm."

The Samarai knew,
Ready for the kill.
Yet they found pursuits
The mind to still.

Look for clues,
The hints are there.
What do you have for others?
What to share?

The test is simple.
If you must ask,
"Am I getting old
Doing this task?"

Stones
Winds
and Life

THOUGHT FORMS

Thought forms are not the truth.
They are limiting.
It is like believing you can see forever,
But this is sight only.
The fog of the thought form surrounds.
It distorts reality.
It often gives no clue to notice,
But like the stack of cards,
There is a delicate balance.
Watch where you put your energy.
The ego will deceive you.
Look closely for the symptoms of belief.
Examine.
Strive to rid your house of these pests.
It takes time.
You must first realize that they
Are not part of you.
Taking a thought form as truth
Causes you to operate on it,
   To be reactive,
   To be judgmental,
   To be critical,
   To be fearful.
Watch for these.
They will keep you running in circles,
Hiding in the cave when the sun is out,
Forming the pile of balls,
Always gathering,
Trampling others when the harvest is plentiful,
Wasting energy.
Notice the true nature of things.
Seek the miracle of your being.
You are meant to be clear and at peace within.
Love and good health,
Freedom and joy,
Fulfillment.
Mighty ships are launched by
Cutting the ropes.
   All at once,
   One at a time,
   Strand by strand.
It is within your power to judge the tides,
Feel the energy brought to you by truth.
Then you will see.

Stones
Winds
and Life

CLUES

As I walked
Along the street,
There was a soul
I chanced to meet.

So small and tiny,
The flame left within,
Quite a challenge
On where to begin.

But when in doubt
Which path to take,
It is love
For this soul's sake.

For finding the way
Is hard to explore;
This society's mold,
Too much to implore.

From cradle to grave,
Look at what we're sold:
"The most, the best, the richest,"
Is what we are told.

So finding the way
In God's true sense
Has been sold out
For just a few cents.

Whether for a few cents indeed,
Or millions to heed,
This path will cause you
To impede.

Truth and reality
Are hard to discern,
Difficult indeed to lift
From society's berm.

Look to the heart,
To the love of man.
Inside each person
A soul does stand.

Some are shriveled,
Some are bright.
You must seek the way
Of God's special light.

As a child, you're created
In His eyes,
Innocent and wonderful,
With no disguise.

He does not intend
The rules to bend;
The love of God
Is yours to send.

First, understand
The ego's tricks,
So very easy
To get in a fix.

Next, take the rules
And throw them away.
Take your life
Day by day.

Pause and reflect,
Feel Nature at work,
Clean and pure,
Above society's murk.

So stop and reflect
To find your inner soul,
A creation of God...
Great happiness the goal.

Not riches and evil,
Nor goals and such,
But with God, Nature
And the Universe to touch.

The truth, the truth,
Strive to hold,
Reality's path
For you will unfold.

So while you pass through,
For a second, a day or years,
Let not the greed and evil
Ring in your ears.

Search for the truth,
Put the ego aside,
Welcome love in your heart...
To forever abide.

The spirit of God is not
To trample a poor few.
Has not the gift of life
Been bestowed to you?

So take this cue,
Just as the rainbow's hue,
The love of God
Is You.

Stones
Winds
and Life

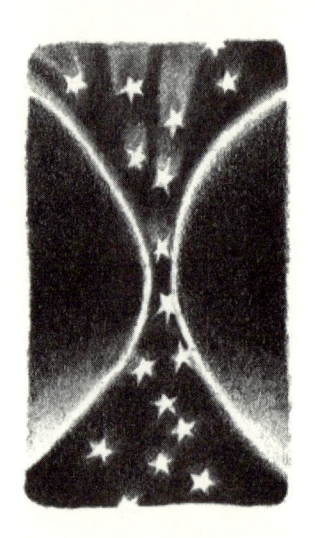

LIFE IS ON TIME

Life is on time,
But maybe we're not.
Have we forgotten
How to walk?

Play back in time,
As children we were,
Malice and ego
Yet to stir.

Looking to innocence,
But being taught shame;
"Break the child,"
From the parent it came.

No longer the loving
Sweetness to hold,
The child is taught,
"Be hard, be cold."

The listening subsides,
The sweetness turns sour.
The authority figures
Are having their hour.

The stillness, the quiet,
Golden from above.
"Lock your feelings
 In the closet, Love."

But back to time,
How does the parallel run?
You can't stop the clock.
Why stop the fun?

The hour glass captive,
By definition it seems.
Be as the Creator,
Use other means.

Open your hearts,
Fight through the pain
From the people who hurt.
Come in from the rain.

Partake of Nature,
Gaze at the stars,
Feel your presence,
How big you are.

Let the hurt feelings come.
Pass through the sorrow.
Harbor no hatred;
It is your tomorrow.

These feelings are yours,
But they are not you.
Conquer the labyrinth
To help you renew.

As large as time... That is You.

DIRTY FEAST

There came upon a midnight dread
A vain attempt to follow the thread.

To grasp at the straw and have it unfold,
To sever its clarity — too bold.

Dancing in the mind in and out,
Too close at times — a very loud shout.

No color — a black & white haze.
Sometimes, it goes on for days.

This escape, this plan doesn't last.
A fleeting comfort in the grasp.

This trail I follow, a twisted end.
For parents' abuse one must bend.

But break not, I'll be back you see,
The clearness, I'll find, it's between God and me.

So exercise your will, enjoy the thrill.
While your mind is inverted, I will be still.

I forgive you, the purpose to be free.
Please go now, far away from me.

Stones
Winds
and Life

PERSONAL

It was thunder and lightning
At the Black Gulch Saloon.
Thelma and Zeke were
Playing that tune.

The cowboy came in
And strode to the bar.
The grizzled beard, the rain soaked clothes...
Told to all he'd come far.

"Whiskey," he said,
In a low gravelly voice.
Something told you
He was not here by choice.

As he shifted a bit
And slowly scanned the room,
I first noticed his eyes,
The reflection of doom.

His movements were slow,
Deliberate and such,
"Spare the Devil
This one to touch."

As he drank slowly
To play his role
I wondered for how many
The bell would soon toll.

As the clock ticked on,
More details did arrive.
This one used more
Than his Colts to survive.

In the darkened room
Of smoke and haze,
The colors he wore
Blended to the maze.

This one was cold
In my mind, no doubt.
He moved to a rear table,
And pretended to stretch out.

Stones
Winds
and Life

Pretending to settle in
With his back to the wall,
He "covered" the door,
The room, the hall.

Then I saw the glimpse,
Which I recognized from afar.
Just under his vest,
Was the Texas Ranger Star.

To his late arrival
No one paid much heed.
The chillness of death
Would precede the deed.

Songs played on.
The cards they were dealt.
Into the quiet corner,
This cowboy seemed to melt.

I thought we'd be spared
A grizzly scene,
But the horses arrived
With the new dawn streams.

The rain had stopped,
But you could hear the wet patter.
They rode slowly,
Sensing something was the matter.

They stopped at the door
And took a long look around.
Satisfying themselves,
One by one, they dropped to the ground.

I heard one exclaim,
"It looks okay!"
He was the first to die,
On this newborn day.

The second one shot,
Stiffened upright with a jolt.
The ranger finished the rest
Before they could bolt.

So through the gun smoke,
The sunlight shown,
Only to be greeted
By a slow death moan.

It was thus I learned
It is not all surprise.
To this day I can still see
The look in those eyes.

Whether or not
I saw vengeance or pain,
In the end,
The outcome the same.

"Personal," he said,
"Now the past is put to bed."

IN THE MOMENT

Fretting and regretting consumed the day.
"Alas," I said, "is this the way?"

So I looked to God and He said,
"Behold, you were not meant the past to hold."

So look, my sons and daughters too,
To be in the moment, it's right for you.

Think not tomorrow or days past.
It is in the moment you must grasp.

Loud and clear the moment rings.
Analyze not the epicenter of things.

Be in the moment. That is joy,
Like a child whose gift is a brand new toy.

Fret not the future
Nor regret the past.

The joy is now;
Practice this task.

DIMENSIONS

Through the line
Infinity came.
Watch the cosmos play this game.

Stand at the vortex
And behold
Clues to the lost ones do unfold.

Believe ye not
The ground is firm.
The Mother Earth yet will squirm!

The eye beholds
What you see,
Three dimensions only.

Feel the air
When it is still;
Expand the senses beyond the will.

Do not things
For others to approve.
Forced tasks do remove.

Listen for the sound
That is not there,
Like the edge of sight to compare.

Sense Nature
As part of thee;
Strive to feel that which you cannot see.

The Universe emits
A distant hum;
To consciousness let this reality come.

The granite —
The rock of solid knowing —
As clear and pure as softness snowing.

Travel through time
Is simple indeed.
But the equations have yet to plant this seed.

Beyond the flesh,
Through the eyes,
How many times has this one seen the sunrise?

The mind is all knowing,
But trapped for some.
The place, the learning, differently come.

In clear light
The prisms break,
Finding the hidden dimensions, the path to take.

Stones
Winds
and Life

HUMILIATION

From the edge of stillness
The chill wind suddenly blows
Across the midsummer's prairie.

It is an evil wind manifested in
The past. It appears from nowhere
Suddenly and fleetingly.

The past was once of freedom and wild herds,
The native man's peace
With Earth, solitude.

Then came the avenger who
Destroyed the herds and
Humiliated the native man.

The cold wind is for the humiliation.
This is degrading — to the very soul,
Worse than killing.

The Earth and Wind take and scatter the dead corpses,
But not the humiliation. It stays with the soul
And must be repaired.

The wind blows over the prairie and penetrates all.
In the warmest most comfortable day
It sends its chill as a reminder.

This is a contrast of existence for all to heed.
The souls of those who inflicted the humiliation
Are in the wind.

They try to get free by absorbing
The warmth of the grasses and soil,
But they cannot. They are part
Of this wind for many lives.

One day they will be free,
But not for now.
This is why they come from the stillness
And the wind appears only briefly.

Stones
Winds
and Life

They cannot come during times
Of joy, love, good health, freedom and laughter.
They may only exit the stillness and
Appear when they will have no effect on any living soul.

Thus in the wind they are taught
The preciousness of others.
When you're on the prairie and watch
The grasses dip suddenly,
And feel a hint of coldness,
Send a prayer after them.

A HOLE IN MY SOUL

There's a hole in my soul,
And the clouds have crept in.
It's a pitch black night
Where the stars should have been.

The moon beams are gone
And like meaningless verse,
My thoughts are chilled.
It is for this day... you never rehearse.

My true love is gone,
Taken from me.
The angels have come;
Now the truth I must see.

Trying to absorb
The suddenness of death,
The sobbing is there
With all of my breath.

Wondrous it may be,
Where my Love has arrived.
We must all remind
That God has not lied.

The pain of separation,
As a reminder of His might,
Will be calmed with time.
I know of the coming night.

At the end of my journey,
I shall arrive there...
Again to stroke
My angel's hair...

Again to stroke
My angel's hair.

YOU CAN'T HIDE

Wow, what a night!
The loved ones are gone,
The moon is bright.
Here you sit wondering what tomorrow will bring.
You don't notice it at first.
It creeps in very slowly,
Just a slight twinge,
Then it grabs and
Wrings you into a sweat,
Starting from the inside, then out.
How many days or times before it's gone?
The gripping is so immense,
There appears no end in sight.
The suddenness is what's so disturbing to the soul.
The day will be going perfectly,
Then the back of your mind opens up and you feel it.
The utter, complete emptiness of it all.
A place you don't want to go
    but there is no choice.
It paralyzes your guts and echoes hopelessness…
Again and again.
Why? Why? Why?
The body compensates and helps the soul with sobbing,
Sometimes uncontrollably so,
Other times soft and measured,
    almost whimpering.
It surfaces in conversations,
    sometimes coming from nowhere.
Other times, on a look or a gesture from another.
A place, a song, a flower, a scent, lingering, pulling it out.
The triggers won't go away
    and you can't hide.
The mind and soul work just as well in the dark, in the quiet.
And that's what you must avoid —
The quiet.
But it's impossible to do.
No amount of friends,
No amount of prayer, it seems,
No amount of words.
Just a time to heal,
A time to soothe the opening,
To pull away from it,
To leave it in the distance
But not to ignore it.
To repair it,
To start anew.
Maybe tomorrow.
Maybe not.

Stones
Winds
and Life

TAPS

It's a sunny day in the jungle.
The animals are gathering for an important meeting.
A truce has been called for the betterment of all.
Lookouts have been posted on the perimeters.
Signals will be given should the man hunters approach.
It is not a happy day.

Many who came to previous meetings are not present;
They are dead,
Killed because they were trophies for ego,
Killed to be dissected for body parts, horns and tusks,
Killed for their hides and skins.
The body count will be tallied.
Those that cannot be accounted for are most probably
    on display in the staring cages or
    perhaps doomed to those places devised to test and alter...
    one of the worst fates of all.

Some have come a day or so early.
Some are just arriving.
Some have sent others in their stead,
    having been unable to cross a large body of water
    or circumvent high mountains or thick pockets of humans.
The sea creatures have counseled with the land dwellers to represent them.
One by one they come to the gathering.
The greetings are with the eyes and perhaps
    a small nod of recognition.
The representatives of each species
    take their information to the record keepers,
    and then take their place in the growing circle.
Overhead the birds glide on the wind,
    landing silently and skillfully in the huge tree tops.
They too act as lookouts.

Stones
Winds
and Life

This is the way it has been in the past,
For centuries before.
But this meeting somehow is different.
As the hour to start approaches
A chill is sinking in.
This meeting was called as a prayer vigil.
Some had said "Not necessary."
Some had said "Foolish."
Some had said "It isn't so."

But now they all know it's true.
Even those who doubted are
Silent with eyes to the ground.
No one looks at another.
The birds sit motionless in the trees.
The wind has stopped.
For just a moment it's as if
The entire Earth is completely still.

The meeting is started just like before
Over the thousands of years
Long before man.
Started very quietly.
Started without the Tiger.

LAST CALL

The wind caresses the autumn leaves.
One by one they float gently to the ground,
    finding their last place in time before decay.
Brilliant reds, rusts, translucent yellows,
    some still with touches of slight green.
They all meet to form Nature's carpet,
    perhaps on concrete, a grassy knoll,
    or in the forest amid Nature's finest.
Soon they too will become hard and
    crisp in the final death.
The signal of a dormant time,
Nature sleeps.
Rejoice in this beginning slumber.
The life part is past, but the brilliant hues remain,
A last call to the beauty of the living.
Hold the colors in your memory
    like the past moments to cherish with loved ones.
It's Nature's tapestry, a final bugle call.
Take it in.
Feel the joy of what you are given.
Preserve the moment.
These are the gifts.

GOOD

This is the day we dread.
We are putting the father
Or mother in the final bed.
There are feelings left unsaid.
This is the day we dread.

So simple to undefine,
Deviate from the line,
All heals in time.

Search in the forest,
Repast by the sea,
Feel the breath —
It is all part of thee.

TOM

Dear Mom and Dad,

The threads are there,
Dangling for me to reach,
But I cannot.
My mind leaps
And I have one for a moment or two,
But to no avail.
They lead to nowhere.

I see the battlefield and faces.
Faces — too vivid!
A long row of faces
As if to parade in front,
One by one.

They're smiling, joking, bantering.
Most have helmets and clean collars.
Some are smoking,
All are happy,
Consumed with the joy of the moment.

Real memories from another time.
I remember hearing their jokes.
Some are repeated now as they pass.
I can make them stop or continue;
It's my choice.
I didn't create them,
But I remember them.

The voices are correct for each face.
Sometimes, but not often enough,
My family passes by.
My mom, dad, brother, sister...
"Good luck."
"We love you."
"God be with you."
Warm farewells,
Laughter at the last dinner home.
"Bravo!"
They are fleeting
And come just about any time.
The others have an echo about them,
Not a real echo,
Just a distantness from where they come.

Sometimes, if I try,
I can bring them really close,
But not for long.
It takes too much effort.
Most stay a few feet away;
That's the way I want it;
It's my choice.

I REMEMBER THEM AT THE CARD TABLE,
IN THE FOXHOLE,
AFTER THE FORMATION WHEN IT WAS OKAY TO LAUGH AND JOKE.
IT'S THE WARMTH I WANT,
THE HUMANNESS,
THE EYES,
THE EXPRESSIONS OF JOY,
GRINS,
WINKS,
THOSE TINY LITTLE NUANCES THAT MAKE EACH DIFFERENT.
LAUGHTER.

THESE MOMENTS ARE PRECIOUS
AND I'VE CAPTURED THEM FOREVER.
THE HARD PART IS NOT GOING FURTHER TO THE FATE.
IT'S A DOUBLE-EDGED SWORD.
THE END WILL FOLLOW EACH
IF I LET IT.
SO I PRACTICE THE GOOD,
DWELL ON IT;
SOAK UP EACH.
THEIR END I MINIMIZE WITH A SHORT PRAYER.
SOME I DIDN'T KNOW TOO WELL,
IN FACT, FOR LESS THAN A DAY.
I GROUP THESE TOGETHER.
IT'S AS IF WHILE I STILL LIVE
I CAN HELP THEM GET TO WHERE THEY'RE GOING.

THE OTHERS, FRIENDS AND MATES,
STAY LONGER.
ONE ON ONE,
MORE PERSONAL,
CLOSER.

THAT'S WHAT I WANT TO SEE
AND MY WISH IS GRANTED.
LIFE. LOVE. JOY.

SOME BRING MESSAGES:
"GOOD LUCK, TOM."
"HEAD DOWN!"
"SEE YOU IN HELL."
THIS IS MY SANITY.

THEY CANNOT TAKE THIS FROM ME.
BUT IT IS HARD;
THE LACK OF SLEEP BLURS THINGS.
I DON'T KEEP COUNT;
TO COUNT THEM WOULD BE TO MINIMIZE,
TO GROUP,
TO BE A STATISTIC IN MADNESS.
THEY ARE ALL PRECIOUS.

Stones
Winds
and Life

THEY COME AND THEY LEAVE.
I AM THE GATEKEEPER FOR THEM;
THAT IS WHY I'M STILL HERE.
THE PRAYERS AFTER THEM HELP IN THEIR JOURNEY.
I DON'T MIND THIS JOB.
MAYBE IT WAS MY CHOICE TO DO IN ANOTHER TIME.
BY SENDING STRENGTH AND A PRAYER AFTER THEM,
I TOO GAIN STRENGTH.
NOT A LOT, JUST ENOUGH TO KEEP ME GOING AND ALERT,
TO STAY ALIVE UNTIL MY JOB IS DONE.

I HAVE THOUGHT I'D RECOGNIZE MY REPLACEMENT WHEN HE COMES,
BUT SO FAR HE'S NOT HERE.
MAYBE I'M NOT SUPPOSED TO KNOW HIM.
I DON'T THINK THEY DID EITHER,
BUT MAYBE THEY DID.
THE ANSWER WILL BE IN THE EYES.
IF ONLY I COULD SEE THE EYES MORE CLEARLY.

I CAN SEE THE LAUGHTER AND THE TWINKLE,
BUT IT GOES NO DEEPER.
I'LL KNOW WHEN I SEE THEM AGAIN.
IT'S PROBABLY NOT LONG.
I SEE MANY NOW AS IT IS.

THESE ARE THE GIFTS TO ME.
THESE ARE THE GIFTS I GIVE.
IF YOU NEVER SEE ME AGAIN,
THEN AT LEAST YOU KNOW HOW IT WORKS.
IF YOU DO SEE ME,
THEN YOU'LL HEAR SOME GREAT STORIES
ABOUT PEOPLE,
ABOUT GOODNESS...

LOVE,

TOM

Stones
Winds
and Life

OMEN — 30°

As I came at once
To the beginning of the great sand,
I stood where giant trees
Did once stand.

For bitterness and hatred
And stubborn conviction to unsettle,
The Earth had been torn
By violent man's mettle.

The barren wasteland
Where many did once live
Is reduced to bomb dust
The size of a sieve.

But alas! Alas!
This toll was not the only to take.
The Mother Earth had decided
Events to remake.

As we stand today looking into the past,
We reflect with awe.
How quickly the Earth did react,
So decisive, so fast.

In the blink of an eye
As warring man ran amuck,
The Earth has acted
And now we are stuck.

Answer me this,
"Why is it that where the sun did once rise,
Is precisely today
Where it sets in the sky?" (30°)

The storms now encircle
With erratic intent,
Drowning out even
The bombs of man's invent.

The Mother has spoken
"ENOUGH! ENOUGH!" she has said.
"The warring must cease,
It is *me* you must now dread!"

"Man did tarnish
And blister and bake.
These changes have come
To lastingly awake."

Agreement be still,
Compromise and love be damned!
A terrible spiral has been
The path of man.

So there was no choice
The violence to still.
Man created this path
With his free will.

For those who remain
After the storm dies down
No longer will love of each other,
Be treated as the clown.

Honor each one
As his soul finds its path.
Let us begin again
Having experienced God's wrath.

Stones
Winds
and Life

Stones
• 40

SHADOWS OF DECEPTION

There came a horseman
So bold to see,
His shining armor
Blinding thee.

Look up, look up,
So fit and strong.
A champion of the times
Never to do wrong.

Strong and swift
He covers the land.
In all the kingdom
There is no more gallant a man.

But look my people,
As the sun does set,
There appears from his shadow
One we have not met.

The last shimmering rays
Show sockets for eyes.
Something is different
For all to realize.

The image has vanished,
The tale is undone!
Fooled by glamour;
The deception is spun.

Did you not think
That to the soul we must look?
The glitter, the shine,
Full advantage it took...

Carved of deception
Now the truth to hail,
The sight now before you
Caused to pale.

Now a mere man,
Touched by a deed,
Soon to be planted
Amongst the weed.

A tale of old,
"Impossible!" we say,
Yet these events unfold
This very day.

The fame is hollow
And the shame as well.
So what more then
Is left to tell?

Forgive the skeleton
In the armor to rot.
Let the rust precede dust
In our strange plot.

Forgive the acts
So we are free.
The good and bad
Are our company.

Our journey to see clearly
Is often clouded and torn.
"Look there,"
Is the seeing man's scorn.

So trust to the heart
Which God gives each.
Search for the truth
Not to impeach.

Each twist in the trail,
Each man fallen down,
Seek the completeness of love
With forgiveness the crown.

THE OTHER SIDE

Here's to the one who was,
Here's to the one who does,
Here's to the one who could have,
Here's to the one who should have.

They come and go,
Their spatters to make.
Buy a diamond,
Bake a cake!

"Sink the Bismarck!"
Sail a ship!
Life flies by
At a fearful clip.

And when it is done,
From diamonds to dung,
Back you'll go to the essence,
From which you have come.

The return is not hollow:
From simple muck
To great experience,
The learning has stuck.

Praise thee on Earth,
The moments to spare.
Do not worry,
Do not compare.

"To the other side,"
As Jim would say.
He knew that
Before his day.

Therefore your life
As the flower grows,
Comes to the final stalk,
From the beginning sow.

Experience it all
As the invisible breath.
The grave is not real,
As the final rest.

OUTLAWS' END

What do you say this day,
To those who have fallen along the way?

Has the faith subsided
As others chided?

Gone is the prophecy to behold,
The hunter about to step from the shadows so bold.

Flesh and bone so easily torn.
From his revolvers, destruction is borne.

In the flick of an eye against the sunset sky,
The outlaw gang about to die.

"A hired gun," there was no doubt.
"NO!" was the last heard gunman's shout.

Rustlers and murderers who knew no shame,
For the bounty... was he to blame?

Writhing bodies about to lay bleeding in the dust,
Quickness and surprise for this stranger a must.

The meal and drinks in Kate's Saloon,
Had left them senseless to the coming doom.

Out in the night to celebrate their plunder,
Shots so quickly they had no time to wonder.

What does it mean this moment in time?
The seconds as hours,
And the thuds as earthquakes,
Stop the dying for heaven's sakes!

The spirit is gone,
The body remains,
So for mankind...
Any gains?

THE LOST SOULS

Came the soul
Unable to meet
The blackened soil
At his feet.
In the blink of an eye
With the lick of his tongue,
His scorched earth policy
Had begun.

"The poets for naught,"
The lifeless he cheers,
"Scorn to God,"
He boastfully jeers.

An age of destruction
He begins to wrought.
"Destroy them all!" He shouts.
"Why not?"

From the charred remains,
To the barbed wire of pain,
In between the fires raged,
Again and again.

"You can take the bodies,
You can destroy the race!
Prepare yourself
Our souls to face!"

The acts, the deeds,
A terrible chill.
Hard for the Universe
To stand still.

So short in time
As compared to all,
Into this chasm of darkness
For light years as if to fall.

Deeper and deeper
Into the history of man,
This blackest hour
Does expand.

Tighter and tighter,
And faster it goes,
Until there is nothing
The horror can hold.

The hurt remains...this terrible pain,
Small in one, large in another.
The souls of many
It tries to smother.

Those who created
This terrible pyre,
Now watch our souls
Through the fire.

They do not burn
As you might think.
So as to miss no one,
They cannot blink.

The procession is endless
And though we forgive,
We are sad for them,
They shall never again live.

Their souls are in shreds,
As if from a blow.
Pray for them please.
They're in hell.
Now you know.

MASKS

It will come to pass
On a particularly foul smelling day,
Mankind will say, "Enough! Enough!
No more to slay."

The stench is so bad,
The air so foul,
We've buried enough pieces
With the trowel.

The grave diggers they knew
From centuries before,
The uselessness of the chains,
The torture, the gore.

Slaughter them all,
Annihilate the race!
Take off the masks,
Look beyond the face.

"Take off the mask;
Not what this seems."
"I'm better than them,
I'm a man of means!"

We fight the cancer,
We replace the hearts,
"It's a big deal," the headlines read,
"Politico farts."

Look to the person,
The real soul there.
Carefully remove the color, the thread,
The society air.

Slowly and softly
On a distant day,
Mankind will remove these masks,
And put the hate away.

Take off the mask
And look to the eyes.
Past the filters
Which have caused this disguise.

Put there by teaching,
By infesting, not fate.
Hatred and extermination,
Are but a few served on this plate.

So simple so far,
Is this not true?
But there is another trick,
Brought by the deceptive shrew.

Inside the mask is
A complicated array.
There is even a mirror,
Looking *your* way.

What does this mean...
To scorn so much?
The mirror is there
To keep you in touch.

It is not complicated,
But you must understand:
Use the mask,
And you too will be damned.

Not to hell,
But to the beliefs you project.
These are mirrors indeed
Of your own private wreck.

Those who hate
Have much fear.
Remove the filters,
Remove the mirror...

FORTUNES

What have you got when you are gone?
What can you tell me for a song?

There are no fortunes which to take
So listen up for goodness sake.

Who comes back from heaven to tell
What they found at their bell?

Can you suppose to buy a spot?
Tell God, for money, to like you a lot.

So look, my friends, not to the end,
But how on Earth the time you spend.

As the sun breaks the horizon each day,
Feel the energy sent your way.

From within, not from without.
Put the man toys like garbage out.

Walk through the forest, towering and tall,
Touch the desert as the sun does fall.

Relish the space, the bliss, the peace.
Devour it not like a feast.

But savor the still, the quiet, the chill.
Enlightenment is not like taking a pill.

Embrace the Universe as part of your thread,
As Nature is part of us, quietly tread.

Awaken your being these wonders to hold,
From moth to butterfly you may behold.

So look not to walls or artificial cheer.
It is your feelings, senses and mind to clear.

Grasp not the quick, the loud, the bold.
Your being's the most cherished creation to hold.

Listen in quiet, perceive in mist,
Feel it unfold as the new flower does untwist.

To others, then, this message please send:
The end.

THE HORSEMAN

There came the horseman,
Dead at last,
But still erect
In the saddle's grasp.

In the end
As he had lived
He seemed to say
"I cannot forgive."

He passed on his horse
With a slump of his head.
His body stiff with vengeance
As if he weren't dead.

"Forgive not, forget not,"
Was his battle cry.
But now there lies nothing
Between his soul and God in the sky.

What do you think
God then had to say,
To this warrior of hate
Who has left us this day?

"Take a comet to hell,"
His enemies would bemoan,
"But for the fleetingness of life
Has the Universe shown."

"Learn not to cast
The very first stone."
Could God have forgiven
And welcomed him home?

Judge not
And carry no grudge,
Lighten your soul
For the final nudge.

When the end swiftly comes
And you're feeling no pain,
Carrying a vengeance
Is a very great drain.

Say no more against,
Seek truth and forgiveness this day,
And with a prayer,
Let us speed this warrior on his way.

His journey of might
In contrast to the fragile flower.
Has followed a scheme
Cradled in God's power.

THE AWAKENING

Dying is hardest on those you leave behind,
You're in Gods hands, no cares on your mind.

You're through the vale...
Old friends you hail.

The living you leave,
Hoping reality to them will not deceive.

A muffled voice as you leave
The fourth dimension you achieve.

The tunnel of light carries you there
The whisper, the quiet, the love in the air.

Bliss from the Almighty, peace from above
Knowest you now, God's pure love.

The body you leave for them to mourn
To adjust to your passing, like a still trumpet horn.

You're free at last, it is hard for them to tell
A few wish you'd gone to "Hell."

But surprise, surprise, you'll welcome them in time
They've finished their paths; with God's light, they too will shine.

As innocence of children, so we strive
Let us not judge, nor contrive.

Trust in God, let your inner soul sing
Be not afraid of this "dying" thing.

Feel the closeness of Nature's being.
It is no accident without the eyes you're seeing.

The Universe is there.
Close your eyes in quiet and sense its presence as air.

So as you live, sense the clues of God's might.
The love and softness shall welcome you on your last night.

Look to Nature to see the trend.
In the stiffness of death the soul does not end.

Your being, the essence of you,
To Nature, to the Universe, to God be true.

Stones
Winds
and Life

ECHOES TO REMEMBER

Clip clop…clip clop
The event is over now.
But the passing of the caisson echoes in the mind.
The sound of loss is loud.
The people were so very still.
Slowly, yet relentlessly, it passed
As if to call attention to a part of life itself.
Blessed are those that could not hear it.
Perhaps their hearts were torn in a lesser way.
To shut out this reality — impossible.
The immense heaviness of this sorrow on each is simply inescapable.
"England's Rose," Mr. John said.
This life bringing so much compassion and truth,
Quickly plucked before the world's very eyes.

As she leaves more magic is cast.
She saw each as a precious being, a child of God.
Next time in lack of compassion,
Remember the silence.
Next time to judge,
Remember the sounds.
Next time to love,
Remember her smile.
Thank you, Princess Diana.

Stones
Winds
and Life

SEEDS

In contrast to his shining armor
    the king's knight looked at the poverty of the village people.
If these are the king's subject,
    then why are they in such a state?
These are the very foundation of the kingdom,
    in poverty and wretchedness?
This did not make sense to him.
For all his years, he had looked at the king
    as unerring, the ruler, the sage.
He had trained well for his part,
    battle strategies, swordsmanship,
    etiquette of council, on and on...
Hard training to properly represent his king and the kingdom.
But this trip was somehow different.
He was traveling slowly,
    taking in the essence of discovery.
He was feeling their pain,
    the wretchedness, the despair.
Except for a few rich landowners,
    the kingdom was in disrepair and poverty.
The people had no hope.
He could see it now in their eyes.
Their souls are not wrapped in fine clothes with full stomachs.
Despair had been a word he used to describe the plight of his victims in battle.
But now he was seeing it in innocent people...starving families.

The king is not seeing clearly.
He has forgotten the essence of rule.
He no longer honors the tiniest flicker of humanity.
He has cut down the forest and taken the topsoil.
He as created a wasteland of despair,
Nothing for hope to cling to.
It is joked solemnly that his subjects are so wretched
    that disease is passing them by.
The knight must know that the storm clouds will soon rise.
A small wind at first,
    then an almost faintly gathering of momentum,
    ever so wistful, here and there,
Until one day the king will look out
    over his scorched and taxed land and he'll feel it.
He won't see it
    or be able to put his finger on it,
    just a heavy feeling creeping into his bones.
That day he'll know his time has come.
He'll discount it at first
    as an "itchy" feeling.

Some anxiety maybe,
    "Perhaps a vacation for his majesty?"
Long ago he turned this corner
    and history has sealed his fate.
His final days will be spent in his castle...
Under siege,
Unable to tax further,
Unable to ignore,
Unable to reason,
Unable to beg for mercy...
The heaviness complete.

The knight stopped and reached down to give
    a beggar woman his bag of grain.
She slowly emptied the grain into her pocket.
"Thank you, sir, for your kindness this day.
Each morsel will be given to a separate person.
This will be the start of the journey back to freedom.
It is the seeds of hope we have been waiting for.
Each grain is tiny and small
    but taken in the right way will bring strength to each.
It is not the size,
It is the timing.
The tide will turn.
Find another king to defend;
This one and his son are doomed.
Just as you have seen despair in my eyes,
I too have read yours.
With this bag of grain you have defended your king.
Thank you for this."

The knight looked around
And the villagers who had gathered slowly nodded.
For this kingdom, his work was done.

Stones
Winds
and Life

ABILENE

Came the stranger
Who rode from afar.
Forebode of his journey,
His horse was Shooting Star.

Out of the blackness,
To the town he came.
The wind before him,
Warning of pain.

Quiet and still
The feeling came.
The poker players soon
Sensed more than a game.

The piano played on,
But between each tune,
The laughter and chatter
Could not displace the coming doom.

The lanterns and street lights,
Usually soft and warm,
Seemed to cast sharper shadows,
And flicker in swarm.

"Up the main street
And turn to the right,"
How often in his mind,
He had rehearsed this night.

Of the dance of death
He does not repeatedly think,
For he knows what he can do
In the span of a wink.

Instead he has chosen
A simple path,
Practiced his exit
After the wrath.

The streets are still
As if to say,
"Fulfill your mission,
And be on your way."

The town's people are quiet
And inside and such.
The thickness of the calm
For them was too much.

Death in the air,
Some had felt before.
After tonight the new ones would pray,
"Never more."

Around the last corner,
His steady horse turned.
"Surprise beats numbers"
This stranger long ago learned.

No rattling spurs,
No trinkets to beat.
He stopped his horse,
And dropped quietly to his feet.

The veil of calm
On the streets could not hide
The question of tomorrow,
"How many died?"

Soft and sure,
He closed the gap,
Using the shadows
As he had mapped.

As the songs played
And the laughter went on,
A distant thought shouted,
"Not for long."

The clock was ticking,
He'd been there before.
Silently and quickly,
He slipped through the door.

The concussions as thuds,
Until the shotgun was still.
Then the pounding of the Colts,
As he snuffed out their will.

The smoke in the air,
Of sulfur and such,
Six seconds of hell,
For them was too much.

The stranger quickly walked
As he came.
Ever so quietly,
They whispered his name.

The hands of time
As if to stand still,
Allowed the winds of death
The living souls to chill.

The chapter was closed
On a dreadful deed.
The avenger as foretold
On a cold black steed.

For reason, no need.

Stones
Winds
and Life

GENERALS AND PAWNS

It's after midnight now.
There is no moon tonight
So the shadows will not play tricks on my eyes.
I can only listen.
The rain has finally stopped.
So has the slapping of the puddle made by the dying one.
During the downpour the moans
Are drowned out.
But now they come
Sporadically and slowly,
Here and there.
They are left to lie.
Those that cannot be found will be removed at next truce.
The generals on both sides do not like to leave them long,
They do not want us to hear our fate.
Occasionally a round is fired and one of the chorus is stilled.
The flares arrive first,
Then the shadows and movement,
Then the sniper rounds.
It's always the same.
There is no timing.
No allowance for sleep.
Dawn will bring the white flags,
A truce while the remains are removed.
It is fitting to be so tired.
The reality of the task is blurred;
After awhile it is all the same.
For those frozen in stiffness,
Instinct tells who lasted the longest.
The will to live in some is enormous.
They hold on,
In the mud,
Lit by flares,
Flanked by generals,
A chessboard of death.

NO END

Go ye not to the castle,
Let God strike them down,
The voices of those tortured
Through the walls will resound.
Pray for them,
The rack and hot stones
Are but a tease.
What they soon meet
Puts the heavens ill at ease.
They shall come apart at the seams,
Pulled to infinity by the oxen teams,
To a darkness far past the screams.
To a dimension reserved for their parts.

Simply gone.

FIELD OF "HONOR"

The battlefield of honor admits defeat,
Even before the drum does beat.
Light the candle on the dark side of man.
Let God give you the words to make your stand.
Listen not to this poem as words.
Let instead God's love be heard.
Ask for help in these trouble spots,
Your words do not go for naught.
Like the rays of light your prayers are heard.
Let clarity attempt to stop the absurd…

…STOP THE ABSURD!

Stones
Winds
and Life

CAISSONS OF THOUGHT

As I awoke to the beat of the rain,
Like thunder and lightning the caissons came.

Samarai and warriors dressed for the kill.
As a young boy I felt a great chill.

The power of words had escaped them all.
And now the king's mercenaries had answered his call.

Headless and armless many soon to be,
The result of just two who could not agree.

And so it spread, the unreasoning grew.
"What's left for stew!" cried the shrew.

The ego fires thus do burn,
Now no one sits in quiet turn.

Alas, to disagree, a healthy stead,
From reason to depart, not worth the head.

And so the start, which once was just two,
Will soon include me and you.

"To arms! To arms," mere words do fail.
The evil winds blow now through chain mail.

Cut not the silence by a tempering of thought,
"No, by God, look at the mercenaries I have bought."

The moans, the cries, the thud of an ax,
The slowness of slaughter ... a terrible tax.

"My will over yours," is the cry.
"Because we do not agree, for this you must die."

The energy, the scorn, the bodies torn.
Look what giving to violence has borne.

And now as I watch the last depart,
The chill has passed, but not from my heart.

From a word or a phrase, to misinterpret or not understand,
There has grown a great toll, soon to be extracted from man.

Stones
Winds
and Life

TWELVE

The riders came one by one,
Almost silently, the mighty horses
Galloped past the clouds,
Manes flowing,
Powerful muscles,
Effortless splendor.

I sat and watched in amazement.
So did the others.
We had never before seen nor felt
Such a powerful expression or event.

Finally, I called to one of the riders,
"What is it?" I asked.
"What's happening?"

"It's a powerful love forming," he said,
"But it's forbidden by some parts of their society,
So we've been asked to help.
Our job is to assist, so that
All see the truth,
To give the parties stamina so they can overcome
the imposed obstacles."

"Does this happen often?" I asked.

"Not at all," was the reply of another rider who had stopped as well.
"Only about once in a thousand years, their time."

"But this is a very important love and we've been called to assist."

"Whoa boy! Easy now! Steady!
You see, even God's great creatures know the importance of this," the second rider explained.

"But aren't all loves the same?
Or at least on equal footing between the two parties
And God?" I asked.

"Yes and no.
Some loves are fleeting, as needs change so does the intensity,
And the love could be intertwined with the life mission as well."

"But love is love, God's strongest force.
Much has been written on it, speculated on it, and many have experienced it;
A truly divine and soulful state," another replied.

"I agree, indeed, but this love *is* different. We were summoned last night,
And as you can see,
Many riders are coming.
It's truly a great gathering
Of energy and purpose."

"Have you been told more?" I asked.

"Not a lot, just that this is a love that will truly move the Universe. It has been coming for centuries, so to speak.
It is a love that will overcome many obstacles.
It is a love truly from the heart.
A love that many will at first scorn as wrong and persecute those involved.
But in the end, they too will see and rejoice with the couple."

"But hasn't this happened many times before and even today in society?" another asked.

"True. True indeed, but this is special love, truly blessed."

"How so?" I asked.

"It's in the eyes.
That is the only way I can describe it,
It's very deep.
When one looks at the other, it's a sense of centuries, a sense of all knowing,
A bond stronger than the atoms,
As powerful as the Creator and
The whole Universe combined."

"I can feel your excitement," I said.

"We all can," said the others.

"Oh yes!
For each of us to be called is an honor we accept
With great grace and humility."

Stones
Winds
and Life

"How many of you are there?" another asked.

"There are to be twelve. Usually, in time past, there would be one,
Or at the most two…
But this time, twelve. Truly extraordinary!"

"Can you tell us anything more?" I asked.

"Just that it is to be a great love,
The bond so strong and deep that there will be tears of joy for many,
Once they all see the truth."

"Well, thank you for sharing this with us. Is there anything we can do?"

"Absolutely. Send a prayer after them.
It will help us in our work,
And thank you all for when you do."

"But wait! wait!
How will I know them?
How will we know them?"

"You will, friends.
 You will…"

Stones
Winds
and Life

AN OFFER TO HELP

I came upon the once-filled moat,
Deep and wide,
Not fit now
For even a boat.

The castle behind it
In disrepair
Took on a deserted
And abandoned air.

Once upon a time,
Joy and laughter did come.
A vibrant place,
A happy hum.

Instead of the flicker
Of the candles warm,
The curtains now in shreds
From the windows did warn.

Instead of a place
Known for grace and might,
Even the sun could not hide
The feelings of darkest night.

Just then, crossing the drawbridge,
I caught a glimpse
Of a one-eyed beggar
Walking with a wince.

"Tell me, friend," I asked.
"Can you please answer for me,
What sad times
Have beset thee?"

"Oh, times are not so bad.
I'm able to eat.
My life is a joy
Compared to what they did meet."

He raised his cane
And twisted his head,
Crooked his neck
As if to play dead.

"For you to jeer
Very bold," I said,
"It's not good
To laugh at the dead."

"Oh," he explained, "they are not dead.
They are blinded by the light.
They only exist
In the darkest of night."

"The light?" I exclaimed.
"Surely you jest.
Of all the kingdoms,
This was *the* best."

"How true, how true,
But look at the weeds.
A very simple thing
They overlooked indeed.

"Although the lowly weed
Does not provide crop,
It exists in nature,
Soil erosion to stop.

"So you must look at the whole,
See the balance there.
To change this,
Like cutting the air."

"Well thanks indeed,
But I beseech thee.
Has not God then
Brought them to their knees?"

"Oh, call it temporary,
A passing phase.
Soon they'll mature
And grow out of the haze.

"They are learning now
That for all the glamour and gold,
Nothing is as sacred
As the human 'hold.'

"So they do exist now,
But on one another to rely.
Something they had forgotten
Even with the sight of eye."

"For these truths and honesty
I thank you, friend.
Can I help you to a
Destination or end?"

Now the beggar did not answer,
But slowly pulled off his patch,
Winking with both eyes,
He turned and said,
"They met their match."

Stones
Winds
and Life

ANGELS' KEEP

There was a black horse
Who rode on the wind.
Some said he belonged to the cowboys
Who committed great sin.

But others said, "No,
He belongs to no one.
The devil tried to ride him
But off he was spun."

So who is this black creature
Who comes from afar?
So powerful and sleek
The Universe is set ajar?

He rides with the winds,
He circles the stars.
When you're alone on the prairie at night
You know in your heart he's not far.

When you're climbin' the mountains
And you slowly look back.
You can sense the angels there
Tendin' to his tack.

When you're crossin' the stream
And the current's swift and strong,
You know if you slipped.
His help would not be long.

When you're watchin' the sunset
And the wheat fields are ablaze,
Out of the corner of your eye
You can sense his gaze.

When times are tough
And you're drawn too tight,
You can feel his presence,
His incredible might.

Next time it's quiet,
Feel your existence and his as the same.
The energy, the muscles,
The flowing mane.

He's there for you
And he'll help any other.
Grab his mane,
Exit the smother.

Take a deep breath
And whisper in his ear.
Where he takes you,
Have no fear.

He's a messenger of God,
A thunderbolt from the past.
He's a symbol for all
That mankind will last.

You'll feel his love,
This creature of God.
His message is clear,
The bedrock, the sod.

It is hard to describe,
But feelin' it is to believe,
A gift from the Almighty
Never to leave.

So next time you're prayin'
And to the heavens you gaze,
Maybe he'll be jumpin' the stars,
Settin' 'em ablaze.

Or maybe still,
If you're in a state of need,
Look over your shoulder
And thank God for this mighty steed.

CLOSED

It's a cold day in hell
And the devil's about.
He's throwin' gasoline on fires
To put them out.

No one's acomin'
And he's havin' a tough time.
He used to buy souls
For a very thin dime.

He's checkin' his watch
And he's waitin' by the gate.
Somethin's fallen down
With his message of hate.

"Where are the souls?
What's blocked the flow?"
A messenger soon arrives with
A tale of woe.

"It seems Mr. Devil,
It's not hard to explain,
The souls on Earth
Have found a new plane.

"They've found the truth,
The egos are shattered.
They now respect the soul of each;
At last it's discovered what really matters."

Well, the devil just looked
And gave the messenger a wink.
"It's really about time
I was wonderin' what they must think.

"And by the way,
You're invited to join them again.
Without fear of me
We can peddle no more sin.

"So go, my messenger friend,
And tell them I wish them all well.
I'm closin' the doors
On this feared place called Hell.

"I'm movin' to the mountains
To be closer to God.
I've done my work.
I too will go back to the sod.

"They're all enlightened.
No more can they be frightened.
They see it clear.
In my heart there is great cheer.

"At last."

Stones
Winds
and Life

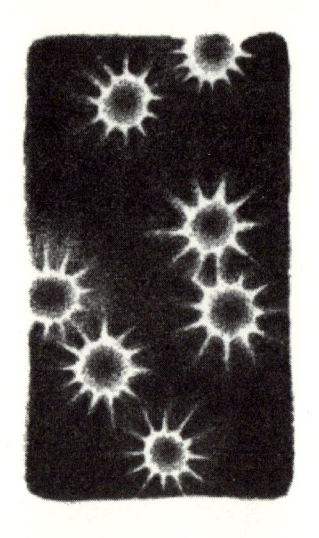

MISSILES

They come to town on a windy day,
Stuffing you up so you cannot play.

Little pollens, little molds,
Too small for little hands to hold.

Sneezy, twitchy, runny nose,
So this is where the pollen goes?

Little missiles, little specs,
To congest my day, what the heck!

Up the nose, down the throat,
Give me a beer, clear the moat.

The eyes water, the tiredness sets in;
Oh my Lord, to be healthy again.

Go to the mall, go to the show,
Let the air conditioning blow.

But sooner or later you're stuck at last.
You must venture outside for another blast.

Run to the car, you won't get far.
With your nose they've scored a par.

The little spores rain down just like hail.
They pound, they dig, they fly, they sail.

Here follows the insight, the secret to fight.
Here follows the recipe to spend a good night.

Balance the body, balance the soul.
Lots of water. Flush them the goal.

Think of this, and ponder the same.
It relates to the Universe, You and God by name.

Good luck

NO TITLE

So where have all the great men gone?
Into politics to become a pawn?

Part of the corruption of church and state,
Many women for which to mate.

Trampling the soul is not the goal,
Not to spy and be a mole.

Following the path of politics before,
"Let them grovel on the floor."

Straight and true never more...
Forked tongue with canker sore.

Hollow in character, hiding their fear,
Angrily they shout in your ear.

Tax and spend to diminishing end,
Into desperation you they send.

"Wake up, wake up, dear sweet prince,
To the world's need do not flinch."

Where have all the great men gone?

BILLBOARDS

Billboards of achievement,
Bought to be seen.
Let us examine
What they mean.

Look at my house,
Look at my yacht.
For other's feelings,
I may give naught.

I've got the gold watch
Ahead of my time.
Into his cup,
I throw a thin dime.

Huge and big,
Audacious and fast,
Stick with me,
Our "friendship will last."

Grab my coat-tails.
I'll take you to the top!
Doesn't my success
Just make your heart stop?

In billboards of greatness
You must believe.
Thus I motivate you,
Like me to achieve.

But let us clear away
The smoke and mirrors.
Try standing around in shorts,
Like "little dears."

If I can keep you in awe,
With mouth wide agap,
I can divert your attention,
And feed you this crap.

My plan is simple,
It is to distract.
Follow my path!
Your money I'll extract.

How do I do this?
You must see me so bold.
I pick your pocket
While my possessions you behold.

Just a little,
Here and there.
I've mesmerized you with
The Billboard Stare.

CaFFeiNE POLKA

I went to the coffee shop to unwind,
Now I got the buzz
I'm feelin' fine.
Two lattes,
A double tall mocha,
On my head I can do the polka.
Rockin and rollin'
Too soon to tell,
Freshly brewed,
I can tell by the smell!
An adrenaline rush in the air,
No fear…no stress…
Hold onto the chair!
Mocha delight…mocha delight…
No way I'll sleep tonight.
Give me a double.
No! A triple I say!
Sleep I must stave away.
Check the grind.
Check the pour,
Will I ever again snore!
Probably not, the caffeine lot,
We're the walking dead,
Buzzing head.
Spend the coin.
Spend the money.
Punch the card.
"Be right there, honey!"

Stones
Winds
and Life

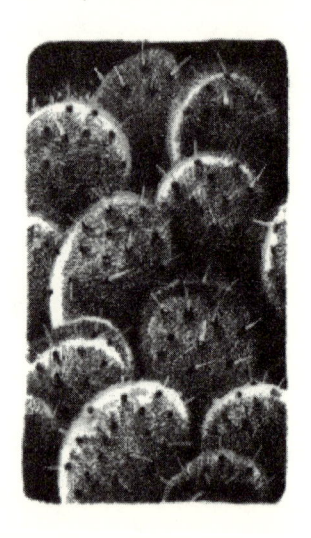

BADLANDS BOB

Badlands Bob
It came to pass,
Was tired of eatin'
Jack rabbits and grass.

His neighbor Nell across the gulch,
Was known for her cookin'.
Not only that…
She was powerful good lookin'!

Thus Badlands Bob,
So tired and drawn,
Decided to get her stew pot
Sometime before dawn.

He waited till her lantern
Grew tired and died.
He'd smelled her cookin',
His nose never lied.

He crawled through the cactus,
He groveled through the sand,
"The lowest," he thought,
"He'd gone as a man."

But times had been tough,
And pickin's slim.
His gold claim
Only turned out tin.

As he approached
He tried to be still,
Somethin' caught his eye,
Movin' on the sill.

Those two round dots
Erupted in a roar
As the salt entered
Each exposed pore.

He rose so fast
He left one boot.
While she was reloadin',
He had to scoot!

Through the shadows
He mistook the way
And embedded himself
In her bales of hay.

Trapped for a moment,
He paused to look and listen.
He heard those clicks
And saw the moon-lit barrel glisten.

Tryin' fast to move,
But to no avail,
The salt was on him,
Like wind driven hail.

He tore through the stack
And headed for the fence.
He was slidin' on his back,
As he first smelled the stench.

He stumbled and rolled
For a very long time.
At least this manure,
She'd not treated with lime.

"I fooled you Bob,"
He could hear her call.
"Watch the cliff…,
I don't want you to fall."

"That's right," he thought.
"The cliff's over there.
Too late!" He felt himself
Floating through the air.

As he hit the ground
He glanced at the door.
When he saw the two flashes,
He knew what was in store.

Through the air
The salt did again rain.
Trying to escape,
He could feel no more pain.

He landed and tumbled
Through the cactus and such.
For a "simple plan,"
This was becomin' too much.

Stoppin' the roll,
He played dead and lay still,
Interrupted, in theory,
By a huge ant hill.

Yellin' and screamin',
He leaped to his feet,
And tore off his clothes
In hasty retreat.

He dodged, he ducked,
He slapped, he clawed.
Why was his plan
Suddenly so flawed?

Out of range he stopped,
To sit by the trail.
The rattler struck his big toe,
As hard as a nail.

But even a rattler,
Can make a smart choice,
The manure between his toes
Was still very moist.

He limped along
To his cabin at last.
He knew he must rest,
Put this night in his past.

Stones
Winds
and Life

Tattered and torn,
He headed for his bunk.
Was it the smell first,
Or the sight of the skunk?

The smell so putrid,
The odor so bad,
He started to laugh,
Instead of bein' mad.

As the shiny new dawn reached
The windows of his shack,
He knelt down in prayer,
"Thank ya, Lord, for gettin' me back."

LET THE CHILDREN BE

Along the way,
As children we start,
From God's gifts,
We are taught to depart.

"Trust not yourself,"
The parents tell,
So they put little kids
Through a kind of hell.

So to yourself listen,
And be true,
For God is within us,
Through and through.

He gives us love
And a wonderful self,
And does not want our feelings
To be put on the shelf.

Tell the adults
To their children be kind.
Let the little ones seek
With their own mind.

Give them peace
And quiet and still,
For their new little souls
Have a wonderful will.

Created by God,
All here to enjoy,
Please do not
Chains employ.

Let the spirit of each
Grow as intended,
For the spirit of the soul,
Shall not be ended.

Save the twisting,
Let the little ones thrive,
So upon completion,
In God's will they'll strive.

Lest ye not forget,
We are all children of God,
Created from yet
More than sod.

We are meant to love,
And we must understand,
Love is respecting the will
And soul of another man.

Love has no boundaries,
No fences, no space.
Let the little ones grow...
By God's good grace.

He answers us all,
Maybe slowly at first.
He supplies what's needed
To quench our thirst.

Stop now
And read this again.
Then ask God
Where to begin.

ANGELS' HELP

There once was a child who knew no bounds,
Wonderment and vibrant,
A heavenly sound.

But she was torn away
By those who believe
You must invest in what you say.

The investment is hollow
And the words are trite.
The angels will help her
Slip back in the night.

Stones
Winds
and Life

HOLOCAUST

They take us away,
Night or day.

Imagine if you can
The ice cold horror
Of being taken from your home,
From your mother,
From your father.
There is no fairy tale...
"Stop!
This is sad!"

The horror is complete.
It is cold and dark.
You are numbed to do as they wish.
Why is this?

The soul is there,
Life remains.
Board the trains.

Caring is right.
This belief comes
The very first night.

This faith from God,
This knowledge, this truth,
Cannot be dissolved.
It is not a mystery to solve.

What a great fear they must have
To create mighty killing factories.
To what end
The murderers they send?

Tiny hands, tiny feet,
Once to play,
Now feel the dead ones
Hardening as clay.

Like the Mother Earth
Through upheaval times,
The landscape is gone;
The bedrock lives on.

Through the rows of wire
The grasses grow.
The evil world of theirs
Cannot stop the "Mother's" flow.

You must contemplate this.
For most probably
This is a time you did miss.

Sit and pause from this world's quickened pace.
Go to your soul and imagine that
You would experience this terror place.
Don't brush it away;
Don't say it's not true.
Let the curtain drop
On your loves,
Your life,
Your existence.

Feel the dark cloud of fear and despair
Grab you by the throat
And thrust you into a blood-curdling world
Of daily death,
Torture,
Sadism and
Pure hatred.

Now stand in the middle of this and ask yourself,
"Why?
What did I do?
What did my mother do?
What did my father do?
My family?
My village?"

Past the furnaces,
Past the screaming place,
Past the sick rooms.
Stand on the bedrock.
To care is the path,
Unshaken by wrath.

To survive is not to live.
To survive is not to be sucked into the vortex of hatred.

From God comes this power,
This knowledge, this will.
So powerful
The screams of death cannot still.

Try as they will,
These people so transfixed by hatred,
Cannot take from us the caring,
The sharing,
The love.

Signed: A small child

Stones
Winds
and Life

EGO WORLD
A play
(Boisterous, Loud, Much Shouting)

JOHN: Welcome to Ego World!
The last place on Earth anyone
Would really want to live.
But many do.

And do they!
Boy! Oh boy!
I'm licking my chops today.
We've got some new arrivals.
Here they come now.
Welcome!

Their parents aren't staying today,
Just dropping them off.
Our graduates often do this.
So loyal to pass it on
To the next generation.
Today, let's go to the judging room.
Hear ye! Hear ye!
Today we judge all.
Welcome all those who are inferior.

Now, here's a problem.
Since this is Ego World
And all are the best,
Who's going to be the Others?
A big problem…
Well, let's come to that later.
Right now, let's get in that barrel
And start judging.
Come on, everyone,
Start pointing, whispering, sizing up.
Be haughty. Turn your back.
Size is different, skin color,
Hair, eyes, dress…
No matter,
Let them have it.

Beautiful!
Climb over them, scorn them.
C'mon, c'mon. Glamour! Glamour!

That's better, great snub.
Look the other way.
Ignore them.
Humiliate them.

Reject them.
Point with disdain.
Great! Wonderful!
Bring up the tempo now.
Remember, someone paid good money for this.
Wait. Wait!
Stop. Stop!
Everybody stop!

What's that little girl doing in there?
And where did she get those flowers?
This is the second time this week.
Three times last month.
It's a virus!
Oh my gosh! We're having an epidemic.
And it's starting with the children.

They're sneaking by our screening process.
They're *giving* away affection!
They're treating others as competent.
They help people feel significant.
No more ignoring.
No more rejecting.
No more humiliation.

Get her out of here
And search the premises.
There could be more,
Remember the little boy last week
With the pet rabbit hidden
In his wheelchair?

Love! Love! Love!
I'm sick of this.
How are *we* going to make a living?
Look here, everyone,
Give back those flowers.
Stop smelling them.
Nature doesn't count;
Banks do.
Compare those balance sheets,
Net worth,
Not gardening…
Wait a minute.
Come back — all of you.

We have more:
Fear…
We have great courses on this.
Be reactive.
Now that's good.
How about adrenaline pumps?
You know, tighten up.
Be the best!
He can't get over me…
That sort of thing.

Being critical!
Wait, don't go.
When you see our poison heart program,
You'll want more.
Come back.
Remember, there's *no* refund.
Don't let the door hit the last one
Of you in the back.
Good-bye.
Try to find another
Hate institute.
You'll see…
[Door slams.]

JOHN: Sarah, are you there?

SARAH: Yes, John, over here.

JOHN: That worked really well, didn't it?

SARAH: Yes it did.

JOHN: Notice how quickly
Love cut through it all?

SARAH: Oh yes.

JOHN: And did you notice
How once a few were affected,
Others followed?

SARAH: Indeed. There were a few holdouts,
But it was truly infectious.

JOHN: Do you think they'll soon forget?

SARAH: Not likely.

JOHN: There were a few tears
When they realized the truth.

SARAH: Yes, yes.

JOHN: Well, let's get ready for tomorrow.

SARAH: If you'll stop by the florist,
I'll go to the animal shelter.
It's hard to keep a
Straight face sometimes,
Isn't it?

JOHN: Yes. (laugh) But necessary.
Faith, Sarah.

SARAH: Love, John.

BOTH: Goodnight…
And bless you all.

Stones
Winds
and Life

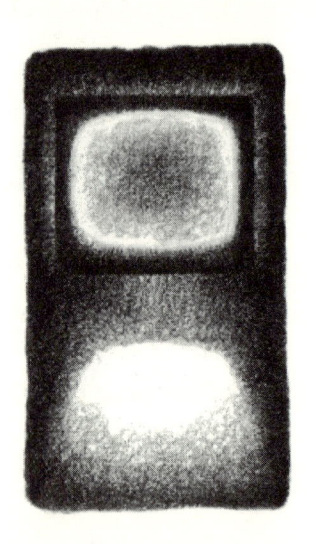

ELECTRIC PARENTS

Turn on the TV,
Pollute their souls,
For the dollar,
This the goal.

Ghoulish and violent,
Blood dripping fury,
Twist their minds,
There is no hurry.

Start them young.
There's more to come.
Show them the way.
Heads roll, "Mere sword play."

Surf the channels,
Saturday morning delight,
Lucky them,
If they sleep tonight.

Instill in them,
A twisted end.
"Blow them in half."
(The body will mend.)

Where is the mom?
Where is the dad?
The channels are parents,
How tragically sad!

So bold are the images,
To a young mind,
"He has nightmares, Doctor,
But not all the time."

Swing the sword,
Chop the ax,
Violence, Violence,
Who's paying this tax?

If you are the boy,
There is not much to hold.
Be strong, Be tough,
Be swift, Be bold.

Your approval will come,
But only if you win.
"Head up, Son,
Take it like a man on the chin!"

If you are the girl,
A different score,
Long legs and short skirts,
"Less is more."

So is it okay,
To maim and destroy?
Flip the channels,
On this baby-sitter toy!

Did you "catch" the commercials,
So tried and true?
Ask them where they want to eat,
Next time they're in the car with you.

The parent, the parent,
It is coming to pass,
Runs on electricity,
And is circuit boards and glass.

Entertain, entertain,
Deaden and numb.
"Gee mom, Gee dad,
Why can't we come?"

WELCOME BACK TO EGO WORLD!
(Loud, boisterous, empathetic)

JOHN: Welcome everyone.
That's it now, children, go right up the steps.
Join the others.
Hello Mrs. Thomas,
Nice "Rolls"
Oh, and your husband has one the same color.
Hmmm, splendid.
Mrs. Cavendish,
What a pleasant surprise.
Yes, nice chrome and lots of it too.
Sent it to England to have it stretched, did you?
Wonderful.
And a new driver, indeed!
Come in now, summer's over,
Time to get to work.
Mrs. Oliver, a new look.
Yes, yes, I see, red,
Fast, two seats, built-in phone, and radar detector,
Six speed and run-flat tires, indeed!
Well...enjoy, enjoy.
Hurry, children, time's a wasting.
The meters are running, so to speak,
Hah! hah!

Okay everyone, line up over there.
Form a single line facing me,
With tallest to my left and down to shortest on my right.
That's it.
Now swing the entire line back so that the tallest is farthest away
And shortest still close.
Yes, yes, I know it's angled,
But we have our new patented, graduated focus,
Depth of field adjustable camera.
Perfect!
Now, everyone facing me, smile.
Excellent.
Another perfect class picture,
Every person the same height, excellent,
For those of you who have put on a few pounds,
Not to worry. We'll adjust your image
With computer enhancement.
No talking please.
Who said that?
Of course we charge your parents a lot.
This *is* Ego World.

No, we're not trying to hide anything.
Listen closely.
We have authority here.
Your parents paid good money for this.
Yes, we are licensed.
Yes, our rent is paid.
The paper hand towels are all you get.
Don't be smart with me, little one,
We've been doing this long before you were born.
Enough, enough, we simply want you to look your best,
Not inferior,
So work on it!
What do we charge for the picture?
Plenty! You little snippet!

If your parents don't pay a lot,
What's it worth? Nothing!
If the price tag is high, it's got to be worth it.
Price tags may equate to real value,
But they may not.
Specifically, this *is* Ego World
And everything is expensive,
Even the toilet paper.
We charge your parents exorbitant prices.
Paying a lot equates to the best
Or so they think.
But I'm getting ahead of myself here.

Well of course.
All you little darlings are worth it, aren't you?
What if your parents couldn't send you here,
Just how would you feel?
Left out?
Dejected?
An outcast no longer associated with this *fine* school?

No, there is no union. I'm the boss.
That is correct.
Some cars do go to the back of the building
To drop some students off.
We'll get around to painting the back,
Sooner or later.
Don't you worry about it.
I'm the valet and I can choose
To open which car doors I want to.
Yes, the front is much nicer,
But most people see that.
I know the plumbing leaks
And I know it did last year too.
It was our decision to put the money
Into the front exterior.
Do you want the world to see you going
Into anything but the best?
Of course not.
What do you mean it doesn't matter?
When your friend is out of the wheel chair,
Then he can come…maybe.

Enough, enough.
This is Ego World.
Attention everyone.
While you are here, I am the government.
I tax your parents.
I make your parents feel good
About sending you here.
Your parents pay a lot and
They brag to their friends.
Remember, bigger is better.
A premise we all may not agree upon,
But many operate on it.
So let's use it to our advantage.
Yes, the building is a wreck,
But look at the front:
Totally glamorous, wonderful.
Let's keep it to ourselves, shall we?
And remember, watch where you step.

You all know it.
Expensive cars drop off at the front and,
Shall we say,
Other "transportation-challenged" families
Drop off at the rear.

              Finally, we have no provisions
              For the handicapped. Sorry.
              This is Ego World,
              A total contradiction in reality.
              And boy, do we make money at this.
              Your parents love to pay,
              So we get you here
              And we give them great pictures
              And mementos,
              Trophies as it were, for their
              Mantels and bragging centers.
              Any more questions?

              Well, the picture makes them feel good.
              You know, "Look he's caught up to the others,"
              That sort of thing.
              You all know how the doctors do it:
              "Well, Mrs. Jones, he's a little below *average*."
              i.e., your poor child doesn't quite measure up to *average*.

              Average, average, average.
              Boy does that suck or what?

SARAH: Oh John!

JOHN: Oh, sorry Sarah, just got carried away.
           Okay everyone.
           Let's give ourselves great applause.
           We've done it again.
           Come on now! Applause, please.
           Why?
           You don't see?
           Look around. Isn't anything different?
           Look closely now.
           Harder.
           You're getting warm.
           No,
           Over there.
           Push.
           Harder.
           Yes, yes.
           It slides.
           Sarah and I built it over the summer.
           A completely hidden room,
           And another entrance from the outside.
           That's right,
           Wheelchair access, elevator if necessary.

Entrance to the bus stop.
Great after hours lighting.
We even have extra clean clothes and
A washer and dryer for those in need.
And look now,
The other students are arriving.
They'll arrive later each day.
Yes, yes,
They pay no tuition.
It's all covered by the amount we charge the others.

Okay, let the others in.
Come children.
Hurry.
Time's a wasting.
Now for a real class picture.
Everyone over there,
Bunch up, no order,
Perfect.
Smile,
Oh, wonderful, thank you.
Now everyone on the floor, or chairs,
Whatever you choose,
Just gather around.
Ready for our first exercise?

Let's start with whoever
Wants to go first and
One by one,
Taking as much time as you want,
And with everyone respecting the others,
Tell us about your greatest experience
This past summer.
And remember the great experience
Can be one word,
One touch, one look,
Something with love in it.
A feeling to the soul.

Yes, yes, recognizing love
When it's not spoken.
That is good.
Feelings of sorrow can be told as well.

              We all agree that animals are
              Wonderful givers of love.
              Okay, okay everyone,
              Not all at once.

              Now who wants to begin?

Later...

JOHN: Well, Sarah, I think it worked.

SARAH: Yes, John.
             Again I say, indeed, indeed!
             A job well done.

JOHN: Do you think they'll catch on?
             The parents, I mean.

SARAH: No. Remember it was the children's idea.

JOHN: I think they've got it.

SARAH: Oh yes, they've got it.
             Now for a little of it to
             Rub off on the adults.

JOHN: It will. Won't it?

SARAH: Oh yes. Faith, John.

JOHN: Love, Sarah.

SARAH: Goodnight, John.

JOHN: Goodnight, Sarah.

COLLECTING

Happiness, happiness,
I beseech thee,
What is necessary
To come to me?

I looked afar,
I collected the car.

Diamonds I gathered,
Bank accounts tethered.

Real estate to hold,
Gold for the bold.

Corporate bonds,
Stocks as ducks on the pond.

Collect and collect
To no avail,
Fleeting of capture,
Like collecting hail.

But then to me
God spoke,
"It is okay
To be rather broke."

The treasure of life
Comes from within.
You are part of God,
So there to begin.

Trust in Him
And what you are.
Each self is meant
To be a star.

Stones
Winds
and Life

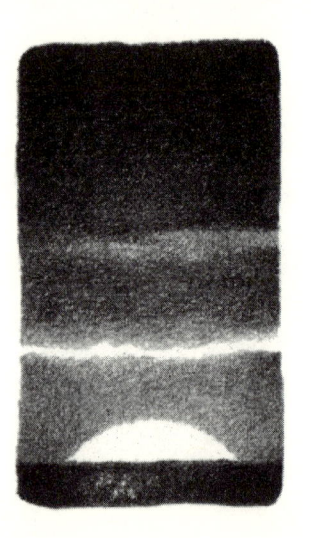

TEXAS TWILIGHT

It's twilight over Texas
And the stars are peekin' through.
The sunset is blurred
By the tears in my eyes for you.

The best thing I had
Is gone like the sun.
And while the night has stars,
My life now has none.

As the sun fades,
My heart grows tight.
The memory of you
Is tryin' to take flight.

You're in my soul,
My being, my breath.
From this hurt,
I cannot wrench.

I know, I know,
I did you wrong.
No pain like this
Has been put to song.

I cannot describe how deep
This emptiness extends.
No word, no song,
This loss of you does not pretend.

The flood of sorrow,
The slow chill of resolve,
I pray in time,
These feelin's will dissolve.

But I know they'll linger
And my heart says some will stay.
It is going to be a long while,
Before I forget the sadness of this day.

This greatest of loves
We once shared with joy,
Is sinkin' like the sun,
On this Texas cowboy.

Stones
Winds
and Life

THE SEA

The sea is quiet...between tides.
It is a good time to visit.
The winds are still,
The smell of freshness will fill your lungs,
These are the times to lift your spirit.
The sea is willing and for this purpose
It will take your burdens
    and diminish your heartaches.
It asks nothing.
You can easily feel its power
    on days of high winds,
        strong tides and crashing breakers,
        but that is physical power...
        a presence of overt and easily-seen forces.
Visit the sea in its entirety,
    accept all of its existence.
You will feel it deep in your being.
Strain as if with a cocked ear to better hear.
Once you are quiet
    you will meet it one on one.
Simply immense.
So huge that to cleanse you in spirit
    leaves not a wake in its vastness.
Beyond the physical...
    a clearing of mind and thoughts,
    a cleansing of the soul.
Come closer and take advantage,
    there is no cost.
Clarity,
A lingering stillness.
If you reach out to the sea
    there will be a matching of energies
    when you arrive.
Pools and eddies to soothe remorse and grief.
Outgoing tides to explore and expand.
Waves and breakers to lift you
    in awareness and thought.
Smells to stimulate.
Any time to replenish.
Gifts.

Thank you.

WINTER

It's wintertime.
The snow gently blankets the Earth,
Soft and pure,
Signaling a time of peace.
The mind and body must rest,
Being close to loved ones,
Sharing simple things,
Taking in the quiet.
The stillness is to remind
That in quiet there is power.
Not power to overcome the will of others,
But the power from within each of us,
The Life Force,
That which we are all part of.
Watch the snow fall.
Each flake,
No two the same,
Adds to the others in silence, peace.
The snow blanket is energy transferred
From the clouds to rest on the Earth.
Picture each flake as a small and wonderful thought.
They build and add;
A peaceful whole.

Look not to the well as a single source of water,
But as a part of an entire process.
Each part adds to the total combination of existence.
The path of the energy and the water form.
Let the understanding seep beyond the analytical,
Silently pass from spectator to participant.
When the time for quiet and reflection has passed,
A new cycle will start,
Softly,
Slowly,
Rejoice.

Stones
Winds
and Life

FORESTS

Walk through this forest slowly, softly,
Like giant mushrooms the trees dot the landscape.
The stalks are long,
Somewhere towards the sky are the tops.
It is as if we, the humans, are the tiny creatures.
Keep walking, quietly now, take it all in.
It is daylight and except for the animals and birds, the huge forest is quiet.
At night, in darkness, they come alive.
It is then that the spirit of the forest makes itself felt,
More profound,
More intense,
An energy of life so solid and immense,
There's no mistaking it.
In old forests a feeling of purity,
Strength, somehow all-knowing.
In young forests it is smaller,
More chatty.
In willowy forests or aspen or alder groves, it is purposeful,
A bit more cutting, direct.
In the jungle under the vast canopy,
It is heavy, weighty, thick, working, producing.
In the desert the mighty cactus are survivors, solid, determined.
Disdain them not!
In oak forests it is spreading and uplifting like expanding the chest,
Taking a deep breath and giving thanks while exhaling.
To each living soul these experiences are different,
Yet all simply magnificent in the entirety.
To cleanse.
To purify.
To enlighten.
Yours to request,
No charge.

PLEASE

It is a quiet day in the forest.
The birds and small animals have left.
The mighty giants await their fate.
It will not come swiftly,
    but slowly and methodically.
The cutters will be working soon.
They start early and work late.
In each case the high-pitched noise will be
    followed by a ground-shaking thud.
The trees are of the Earth.
They are rooted in the Mother
    and extend towards the Heavens.
They are guardians of the land.
They hold it in place and allow smaller life
    to nurture and take hold.
The trees help free man of troubled spirit
    if he lets them.
Many who have walked through the giants
    have felt their presence.
Each forest has a spirit.
After the cutting, the Earth mourns,
    but soon the spirit is slowly reborn
    in small sprouts.
Those animals that can, will return.
It starts anew, but not as easily as the first time,
    or the second.
In times of fire or earthquake,
    it is the natural course of things,
    but the cutting is like an amputation.
The living is abruptly halted.
This causes shock and the spirit
    of the forest must mourn.
The larger and older the trees,
    the greater the blow,
    a more profound effect.
The silence after the cutting is deafening.
The rain falls on stumps.
There is no longer a feeling of life
    reaching toward the Universe.
The nights of activity when their spirits came out
    are now quiet.
There is no more healing for man.
A part of the Earth has ceased.
Can you feel it?
Hollow silence…

Select carefully from the Earth.
Like the fruit trees,
Some are ready to give, others not.
Each has its own cycle.
Listen first.
Walk among them and you will know.
The economic cycle does not hold.
It is created by man, not Nature.
The natural cycle, if obeyed,
    will regenerate and replenish quickly.
Choose carefully, please....

Stones
Winds
and Life

WHITE NOISE

Whitewash it
Spin it
Look the other way
Ignore it
"Couldn't happen here"
It's their right
Bury it
Family secret
"Paper tiger"
An accounting adjustment
Do you believe your eyes or me?
Power of the press
Let sleeping dogs lie
Put it to rest
They know best
He knows best
Mommy knows best
Keep still
"Dummy up"
Dead men tell no tales
With prejudice
Facts are facts
It all points to the direction of…
A "breaking" story
Tune in at 11 o'clock to see how this
New development will affect your life!
"You won't want to miss…"
Physicians recommend…
Family values
Family man terms
Runners up
Second place
Queen for a day
Fit for a king
Subliminal
"Clam up!"
"Stuff it!"
"Tough it out"
The Department of Justice
A worthy cause
Sticky bricks
Hidden agenda
Top secret
Your eyes only

It never happened
The reputed mob boss…
The alleged informant…
News sells
Taken a turn for the worse
Critical condition
Intensive care
Hanging by a thread
Confiscate all video tapes
A slow burn
Napalm
Agent orange
The "G" word
Ringing in the ears
It's a wrap!
Without a trace
A scientific breakthrough
Unfolding events as we speak
My word is my bond
Our books are open
An accounting error
Finish it
Are you still here?

GREAT APPLAUSE

It's springtime.
Nature is awakening from slumber.
Renewal is starting.
The stirring begins.
A long, slow stretch
Feeling the sun's increased warmth,
At first imperceptible,
Then a tiny bud,
The faintest of sprout,
The forest picks up its pace.
The leafy trees' shadows become thicker.
Like a large orchestra,
Each day another instrument is added,
Small and delicate at first,
Followed by medium and more occasional sounds.
Finally, the wonderful mix of all.
Splendid, powerful, gripping.
Nature's virtuoso,
Life in full swing.
Put your hands in the air as the greatest of conductors.
Feel the incredible energy.
Join it.
Be part of it.
Uplifting to the soul.
Pause and reflect on what is happening.
Walk softly, slowly,
A nourishing time.
Delicate.
The softest petal finds it place.
Behold the harmony,
A complete sharing.
The might of Creation
So well thought out,
A lesson to experience,
A gift of immeasurable size,
A bow,
A thank you,
Great applause…

Stones
Winds
and Life

THE KINGDOM

It has been a week since we last visited the park,
    a wonderful place with open fields,
    woods of huge fir trees,
    a small swampy area filled by winter's high waters
    and a lake.
Not a really big lake, just the right size to stroll or jog around.
What a wonderful place for the dogs to run,
    people to stop and chat,
    back to Nature.

The Ruins
I first noticed it upon getting closer to the lake.
I'd heard it was there,
    the old "mental hospital."
It was gray, probably rather large up close,
    but it seemed not too big looking at it from afar.
It sat on a hill, overlooking what must have been
    an active valley in those days:
    wildlife, growing fields, livestock.
Perhaps a fitting place to recover,
    taking in such a view, serene, peaceful…
But today, nature is alive.
People are about,
    a nice day to stroll…
    a quiet adventure.

The Assessment
Rounding the lake and assessing the location of the building,
    it's evident there are two paths to it;
    continue around the lake and up a short way,
    or go up the steep hill and come out on higher ground
    to look down upon it.

A Time To Explore!
The "Child" kicks in…
Up the steep hill like "days of old,"
    wondering what's on top…
    excitement, expectations, pure adventure.
All knowing that once you're there, you're on top,
    the absolute ruler.
The *King* shall overlook his castle
    and all his kingdom:
    the lake, the woods, the fields,
    the spectacular mountain view.
Only *mere mortals* would be so foolish as to attempt
    to venture to this stronghold.

Absolute power!
Rejoice!
I am the *King!*
I am invincible!

At the Top
Straight ahead is a row of trees
    leading to the building.
There it is, slightly downslope.
Evident now is that some walls stand, others are caved in,
    it's three stories, no roof, weathered concrete.
Hmmm, go to the treeline and follow it directly
    or cross the field?

At the Tree Line
A wonderful discovery…the old roadbed leading to it.
The road is indeed lined with trees on one side,
    a stately entrance.
Perfect for "Royalty," even today.

On the Road
Well, "Let's not keep them waiting."
The *King* begins his triumphant return.
The sun is starting to peek through the clouds,
    fitting for his journey.
Closer and closer,
    an easy stroll on the old gravel road bed.
And then it hits…
Slowly at first.
What is it?
A sense not to hurry any longer.
The adventure is gone…vanished.
The air is heavy, thick.
But it's not the air.
It's this place.
Going closer must be done quietly
    so as not to disturb what's here.
Softly now!

In broad daylight on a clear day, the going is hard.
It's not heavy breathing,
    it's one step at a time, slowly.
Feet are heavy here.
Everything is heavy.
Walking here is like stirring the past.

Then I hear it.
Not from the outside in,
    but from the inside out.
The screams!
Don't laugh.
It comes through the soul, wrenches your gut,
    and stops where it can be heard.
There is no chorus,
    just a continuum,
    closer and closer.
What was this place like for so many?

The Building
Some walls do indeed stand,
    others are tumbled.
The entrances remain on either end
    and clearly it was three stories.
Concrete and steel,
    solidly built in its time
    with lots of windows…
    a nice touch.
The entrances are porch-like, rather grand, stately.
Some of the tumble-down concrete is
    giving way to the blackberries.
There's a sign;
    The ruins are being used to practice disaster rescues
    by those who would save us
    in times of earthquake or collapse.
A barbed wire fence encloses it all,
    but it's easy to walk around.
The grounds were probably
    once very nice.
The view magnificent.

Graffiti
A "No Trespassing" sign,
    but it's easy to get in,
    the graffiti writers have a small hole in the fence.
Graffiti: different here as well,
    not cheerful, but sullen, brief
    speaking of death…dark.
Maybe they too felt something,
    a twinge, an uneasiness, a sense of being watched.

Stones
Winds
and Life

Dark Holes
The lower floor —
That's where the screams begin.
An ugly place,
    a dirty rotten filthy ugly place for humans to be.
You do this in the name of science?
Playing like this with sick people?
Turning a blind eye when you know this is going on?
This is a dark hole in humanity,
    a festering boil of a not-too-distant past.
The screams…
The silent screams.

Help!
The *King* stands completely gripped by what he is feeling.
The adventure shattered, as the mirror on stone.
He silently stands and asks Heaven to come and clean up their souls.
Even mighty *Kings* need help.
Today he calls for help.
With all his being, he prays
    that this place be healed by God,
    that the souls of these people who endured at this place
    be cleansed and restored.
The *King* prays that someday he can return to this place
    in silence
    in peace
    in love.

Exiting
Leaving is not easy.
The heaviness remains.
The birds, the dogs, the lake, the people
    do not diminish it.
It's there for a long time.
Only at a great distance
    does it slowly let up.

Back To the Field
Bigger strides,
    sunbeams.
A glance back over the shoulder,
    a very long glance.
The threads remain,
    haunting in a very real way.

Rejoice!
The *King* has looked to the Heavens.
He has asked with all his energy and humbleness this day.
It will be accomplished.
He has faith.
Someone's calling....
    time to go.

Stones
Winds
and Life

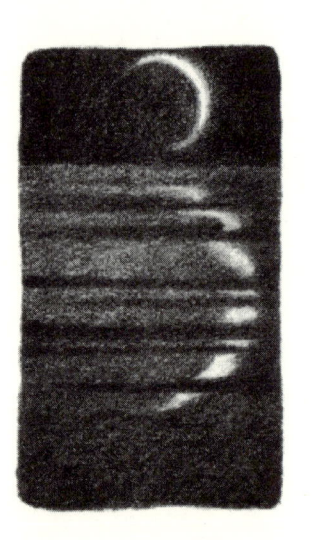

THANK YOU ALL

The moon shimmers across the water towards me,
But somehow doesn't quite make it.

The waves lap against the rocks below,
But somehow the sound doesn't reach me.

The wind gently blows,
But I do not feel it.

I hear my friends call,
But I do not answer.

They have all come to help,
To make me feel alive
When the heaviness and grief
Are so overpowering.

Living through this
Must be the lesson,
Discovering the soul,
Wanting it to go away,
But it's so deep,
So attached.

The world has become slow,
So very deliberate.
Part is as if paralyzed,
Unable to move,
The rest just suffers.

Oh! The tide has risen,
Time to move,
The inevitable has arrived.

Is this not the inevitable,
The end of the love union?

My mind tries for reason,
But cannot move fast.
I simply miss her so…

I don't properly thank the ones
Who've come to help,
But they understand.

The old one's touch,
The look in the young one's eyes,
A universal language
Appropriate for the times.

There's nothing more
That I can say this day,
Except,
Thank you all for coming.

BATTLE FATIGUE

The trucks and tanks just keep rolling by.
Hey! Hey! I'm over here.
It's just too noisy; they can't hear me.
They've stopped. Okay, shout.
Hey! Hey! Over here! Over here!

Darn, the engines are still too loud
And those bushes in the way.
How long have I been here?
An hour? maybe two?
It's hard to say.

I remember the battle, starting just before dawn,
The shelling, the shouting, the confusion in the dark.
Lots of screaming this time.
Someone close to me was hit,
Poor soul. It must have been really bad for him.
Close gunfire and explosions, really close this time.
Lots of shadows and concussions.
Load, reload, down, move, stay oriented, more moving shadows,
Ours or theirs? Down, stay. Move: instincts take over.
The flashes blind, the hearing is numbed.
Now all is slowed. In slowtime, reality exists.
Deliberate; the edge to stay alive.
When you're in it you're going to live.

Hey! Anybody! Over here —
Look, would you —
Good, good, good,
They're looking now.
Okay, come on, see me, that's it.
Hey, don't go! Stop!
Over here.
Strange, they looked right at me
And just kept on going.

"John?"
Yes, yes, you saw me, finally.
Over here. I'm here.
"Sorry we're late."
Boy, I hope so. Did you see those others just looking and ignoring me?
"Well, John, with the shape you're in, you can hardly blame them now, can you?"
What do you mean? Oh, oh. I'm really apart, aren't I...
"Yes, you are, and may we say...*a little hard to look at* might be an understatement."
So you're here for me?
"Absolutely. How's your spirit doing?"
Pretty good, I think. I was really wondering...
"Yes, we apologize for the delay,
Just very busy with the transfers.
Are you ready?"
Yes.

JOURNEYS

Softly now,
They're just around the next corner.
Slowly, very slowly.
Although they cast great shadows,
The sun somehow seems more intense in their presence.
We're almost there.
Easy now,
The footsteps slow in great expectation,
Never to be disappointed.
Before you know it, you're among them,
The giants of the world...
Centuries in the making...
Walk quietly and revel.
Put your hand out and feel them.
They're not close together
Like young trees.
Your eyes have to almost refocus to take it all in.
Even so,
Without sight there would be the feeling,
So solid, such an immense statement from the Creator.

It's like you're standing on soil,
But at the bedrock of Creation.
This is it.
A statement so loud there is no doubt.
No "logic" of man to refute this or shout it down.
It's just there, unspoken, unchallenged
By anyone or anything.
Continue on...
After awhile you're in tune with it,
Part of it,
More comfortable.
Even the smaller life is reverent in their presence;
Not so much chatter, as in young forests,
Just a quiet resolve to exist among the giants.
Perfect harmony, each species
Complementing the other,
An environment in balance,
Led by the Big Ones.

Other: How's your writing coming today?

Writer: Who's there? Who said that?

Other: Well, I'm looking over your shoulder and it looks excellent to me.

Writer: Very funny. Now come out and show yourself…this very minute! Who are you?

Other: Don't be shocked, but we've met before.

Writer: I don't think so.

Other: Oh yes we have, remember the falling limb two years ago?

Writer: I do indeed. A close call, sir. Did you drop it from the sky?

Other: Not exactly, but I deflected it so as to spare you no harm.

Writer: A likely story, but since no one was around and I spoke to no one about it, I'll lay a little truth to it. Now come out and show yourself. Who are you?

Dragon: I'm the dragon of this forest.

Writer: Right! And I'm Sir Lancelot.

Dragon: No really, I *am* the dragon of this forest.

Writer: Forests don't have dragons!

Dragon: Well, this one does — and I'm it.

Writer: So I'm stuck with a dragon, or at least a voice who claims to be a dragon, each time I'm going to visit the King's forest…

Dragon: It's not the King's forest. It's the Creator's, and He put me here to protect it.

Writer: A likely story, show yourself to me then.

Dragon: It takes a lot of energy to do that.

Writer: An excuse I see.

Dragon: No, it really does, the communication isn't easy either, but I've been given special powers today to thank you for your work.

Writer: What work?

Dragon: Your writings about the forest and making others aware of what a special place it is.

Writer: Well, I admit my writings have been well received, but it's an easy job for me, in fact, a pleasure. I gain energy from my visits.

Dragon: Your writings attract others to come and experience the existence. The more troubled ones receive special washes to cleanse their souls and help them on their path to enlightenment.

Writer: So you are an enlightened dragon?

Dragon: No, my real job is to protect the forest.

Writer: From whom, may I ask?

Dragon: From the ones to come, several centuries from now.

Writer: Then what?

Dragon: Nothing special, really, it will just be that no matter what, this forest will be preserved for all to enjoy.

Writer: So, let me recap if I may. You're the dragon who roams the woods protecting it and saving people and you'll be here for centuries to come. Right?

Dragon: Right!

Writer: Honestly, Dragon, I do remember the limb being thrust aside during its descent, so I'll give you that one. But how come you waited this long to make yourself...or should I say your voice...known.

Dragon: You weren't ready.

Writer: Ready for what?

Dragon: You weren't ready to know that you're not alone, that the entire Universe wants to help pull that of God from each soul.
So now you know you are part of a bigger scheme, like all others. Just that in your case, your writings are published and read throughout the land. As a result, more people come to enjoy God's creations in this forest.

Writer: The King's forest.

Dragon: No, God's forest, the King is just the caretaker; he is worthy to watch it in his life, and his successor will be worthy as well.

Writer: How tall are you, Dragon?

Dragon: Oh, about 40 feet.

Writer: Will you always be here when I come?

Dragon: Generally yes, but I may be helping others.

Writer: Will I ever get to see you?

Dragon: Maybe, but it takes a lot of energy to appear in your dimension. I'd rather save it for another day — say a very special occasion — if you don't mind.

Writer: Well, how special an occasion?

Dragon: Very special. Let's just say that your life's journey is by no means over.

Writer: Just a glimpse. Please, this *has* been quite a conversation.

Dragon: Very well, stand very still and become very quiet inside and close your eyes. When you're ready, turn very slowly to your right and open your eyes, slowly and quietly…

Writer: I see. I see. I see. Thank you, Dragon.
Dragon? Dragon??

Exiting the giants is different each time.
Sometimes the walk through becomes
more brisk after awhile.
Other times, the exit is slow,
Deliberate, not wanting to go,
But being pulled by other thoughts or
matters.
Today is somehow different,
    a pleasant task to leave,
    accomplishment is in the air,
    a solid future,
    the giants are intact,
    the forest protected,
    a feeling of solidarity prevails.

Ahh! The final turn out and the view of
the valley below.
Stop and rejoice!
Life!
A glimpse out of the corner of my eye.
"Thank you, Dragon…"

"No. Thank *you*…"

DRAGON'S HELP

Love,
Can it be by itself?
Can it exist as a single entity with no ties?
Can it be captured thusly
And put in a box?
"The relatives" are coming, find the box.
Oh, where is it?
We need love today,
It's a special occasion.
Hurry children, find the box.
Everyone is coming,
Your mother is preparing a special dinner
And we need love.

The leaf floats to the ground
In a time it has grown from tiny bud
And now it seesaws back and forth
On the wind as it falls.
Crash! It arrives on Earth — literally.
Now it is at the mercy of the elements;
Back to the soil if in a forest,
Most probably a candidate to be swept or ground up
If in the village on the cobblestones.
At best to be part of a large pile
That children are playing in,
Tossed to the air, marveled at,
Part of a big blanket,
Or better yet,
A hiding place.
Fun, laughter, good activity,
A last hoorah!

Voice: Well, you're back.

Writer: What? Who's there?

Voice: Very funny. You don't recognize my voice?

Writer: Come out, sir! Whoever you are. There have been thieves running through these forests and I can assure you I'm well armed.

Voice: Oh sure, your sword is so little used and so highly polished, you're going to blind them with the reflection.

Writer: Very clever, Dragon. I assume you've been guarding the King's forest with your usual zeal — something equal to the wit I've just heard this day.

Dragon: Of course, this is one dragon who is never at a loss for words. And incidentally and inexplicably, those thieves you spoke of suddenly decided to ply their trade elsewhere. Their stay, I might add, very short-lived.

Writer: Hmmm. So here am I the writer, who is often at a loss for words, with a dragon for a friend who is never at a loss for words.

Dragon: Yes, and today I see you struggle a bit…

Writer: It is love, Dragon, my mind wanders to capture the essence of it.

Dragon: You're trying *too* hard.

Writer: Really, you say?

Dragon: Yes, sink more into the forest and see what you get.

Writer: "Seeing" what I get? Very cute, Dragon. What I'm getting is advice from a dragon I can't see. Although I'll admit, one with a quick wit and a gentle way.

Dragon: Very well, I'll be serious, or in your case, today *pretend* to be while we talk.

Writer: Thank you, Dragon. So, do you have an answer for me?

Dragon: No, except to melt into it. Find a place comfortable to you, whether in the mountains or by the sea, strolling in the woods, listening to the rain, watching the snow fall, the sunrise, the flowers bloom, hearing a new infant's cry, laughter, finding good friends, harmony, peace.

Writer: Dragon!

Dragon: Yes. Oh, sorry, I kind of got going there, didn't I?

Writer: So Dragon, you're describing life. But you left out the hard work, like what I'm struggling with today.

Dragon: Why are you struggling?

Writer: Because I must explain it, put it to words.

Dragon: Like something so profound that your writing will be read by all — this part on the essence of love? This true definition of love?

Writer: Well, not exactly…

Dragon: What then? Or who is this for?

Writer: For me!

Dragon: Ah hah! So you are in love since we last talked?

Writer: Yes.

Dragon: And you are surprised?

Writer: Yes, it came suddenly and unplanned. A simply wonderful person. It is like I have been sent an angel, so soft, so caring. Her touch and gaze melt my soul.

Dragon: Hmmm. Sounds like love to me. Congratulations.

Writer: Thank you, Dragon. But what about the essence of it, the core?

Dragon: You write too much. Put away your pen today and stroll through the forest. When you leave, take the west path to the beach area. Once there, linger and take it all in, feel the tide pull, the sea breeze on your skin. Watch the sun set.

Writer: Are you saying then that no matter what, I can't describe love? Find the core? Give people something to look for? A definition, so on…

Dragon: Many writers have already done that, each in their own way, some very elegantly, I might add.

Writer: True.

Dragon: How do you feel when you write about the forest?

Writer: It comes from the heart. It just comes out.

Dragon: Is that hard to do?

Writer: No, it's very easy, it just flows.

Dragon: Hmmm, and if you were to write about your new love?

Writer: It is easy also. The words just leap out effortlessly.

Dragon: When you are in the forest and very quiet, what do you feel?

Writer: Very simply, the immensity of it.

Dragon: And when you are with this new one in your life?

Writer: I feel like we are part of one another. I feel immense joy. It is like a magic gift that uplifts my soul. I must still pinch myself to see if it's really true.

Dragon: Then you are telling me that when you are open to the essence of each, whether it is the forest or your new love, the experience is easy.

Writer: Absolutely. For me these experiences are indeed effortless.

Dragon: Do you have other experiences that bring you joy?

Writer: Yes, many. Some I don't write about, but nonetheless I feel joy and happiness.

Dragon: And these too are not difficult?

Writer: No. All I have to do is be open to experience them.

Dragon: Say, to pay attention?

Writer: So Dragon, you want me to give up the idea of the essence of love, put down my pen, experience the forest, watch the sunset and go home?

Dragon: Not exactly, but ask yourself what you find in the forest, what you find with this new loved one, and what you find in all the instances that bring you joy.

Writer: Well, it *is* effortless.

Dragon: And does it bring you energy?

Writer: Yes, I'm always uplifted.

Dragon: Incidentally, I'm glad it is working out with you two.

Writer: You knew?

Dragon: Yes, and so does the forest, and the entire Universe, for that matter.

Writer: My dragon friend exaggerates.

Dragon: Maybe. But tell me again how you feel about your new love.

Writer: Wonderful, exhilarated, my soul sings with joy.

Dragon: And it's not difficult. In fact, it brings you energy as you stated.

Writer: Yes.

Dragon: So maybe you could say that the essence of love is a gift that is effortless in task which brings great energy to the very essence of your being.

Writer: It certainly is nice to have an eloquent dragon who is invisible and who protects the forest as a friend. I shall ponder this.

Dragon: Promise me you won't ponder *too* hard.

Writer: I promise. I promise.

Dragon: Now enjoy the rest of your day and your gifts. Others, I might add, are enjoying the gifts you are giving.

Writer: Thank you, thank you, Dragon. I'm on my way.

Dragon: I know. And you're very welcome.

PASSING

I wipe my eyes
But the rain still falls.

I blink my eyes
But it is still dark.

I hug myself
But I am still cold.

I have eaten
But the hunger remains.

I have cried so much
But the hollow stays.

I feel the wind
But not on my skin.

I hear footsteps
But turn to no one.

I can see so well
But I only stare.

I turn to leave
But can go nowhere.

I can think very well
But my mind will not expand.

I can find the words for prayer
But they will not flow.

I can sense the caring
But cannot grasp the energy.

I want time to hurry
But it is slow to the second.

I want to stop
But I live on.

I believe in nothing today
But know God is there.

I exist
But I mourn.

In the midst of it all there is joy.
This poem is done.

Stones
Winds
and Life

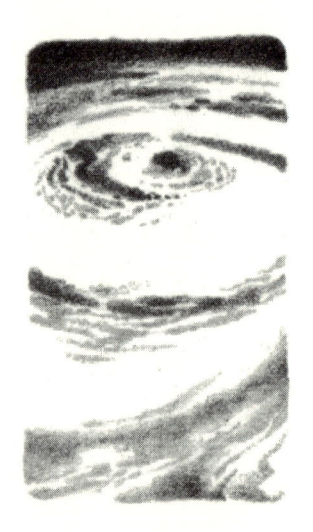

WINDS

The horses and their riders
First appeared to us as tiny specks
In the clouds, then they grew
Larger and larger until they
Thundered past.

Full battle gear...
I looked at the others,
A sight we'd never seen.
Swords and armor,
All designed for easy movement,
Yet serious business,
Too serious for anything we'd
Ever seen come out of the Universe.

As each rode by
We could feel the wake of power
Intense, solid.

Finally an opportunity...
One rider slowed to adjust
His battle dress and
Cinch up his saddle.

       Excuse me, sir,
       Where are you headed?

Rider: I can't tell you for sure
         But we're going back
         In history.

       To a battle?

Rider: Yes,
         In a manner of speaking.
         Or more like a series of battles,
         At least that's what I'm told.

       You've all been passing
       One by one for
       Quite some time now.

Rider: Yes, it takes time
         To gather from all over
         The Universe.

       Do you have far to go?

Rider: I don't think so.
The battles were pretty recent
In Earth time.

Are they being fought now?

Rider: Good guess.
Maybe you saw the
Flashes down there.

Yes, we did,
But had no information
Other than the other riders
Began to thunder past.

Rider: Has anyone returned?

No.

Rider: They probably won't,
For a while at least.

If you don't mind our asking,
Why do they send
Battle riders and not angels?

Rider: Simple, and a good question.
Angels are gentle;
They enhance love and knowledge,
A nudge here and there,
Comfort in times of sorrow.
Messengers of healing when it's needed.
Along the way of enlightenment
They light the candles to show the path.
You know the rest.

Yes, we do.
Indeed we do. (nods, etc.)

Rider: But now, mankind has gone
Too far.
What started as a dispute
Has grown and
Several countries' leaders
Have forgotten how to reason.
They are about to execute
Some deadly force that will
Change Earth for a long time.

Who called you?

Rider: The Mother Earth.
It's as if a great crack
Is about to open in humanity,
If it hasn't already.
The sensing was instantaneous
Throughout the Universe.

Yes, now that you mention it,
We felt something
But couldn't put our fingers on it.
(more nods, etc.)

Rider: Doom!

Doom?

Rider: Yes, doom. Unless
You've evolved more
You might not recognize
The subtleties with which it starts.

I would think that
Doom would be like a
Quick explosion
Or sudden earthquake.

Rider: Not so.
Doom has warnings
Just so action like this
Can be taken by the Universe.

Oh, oh!

Rider: Doom is very serious
And must be interrupted,
This time at least.

Mother Earth knows
You're coming?

Rider: Oh yes.

(A rider thunders past)

Rider: Whooa Boy!

Your horse looks a bit edgy.

Rider: Yes, this is his first interdiction
But he's a good one, trained well.
He won't let me down.

Interdiction?

Rider: Yes. In effect
We'll stop the slaughter and
Add some reason to their plates—
Respect for other souls, you know.

Yes, we know.
But how do you do it?

Rider: Swiftly.
Like the cutting edge of the sword.
If you are close to the edge
You hear nothing,
You see nothing.
Its swiftness leaves traces
Only in the molecules it parts
And then only for a brief moment—
If you know what to look for.

So you are going back to change history.

Rider: Oh yes.

They won't know?

Rider: The enlightened ones will.
They will sense it.
Even to them it will be
A slight stillness,
Like when you're alone
And you feel something.
You know you feel something,
So much that you stop and
Look around.
But there is nothing…
That sort of feeling.

I understand.
In fact, I felt it
Once before on Earth.

Rider: Now you know.

Interesting.
Thank you for the insight.

Rider: You're most welcome.

How long will it take?

Rider: Their time? Several years.
That's why so many are coming,
It's a big job.

I picture many of you,
Swords cutting, effectively altering the events,
Like a large battle with no visible adversary,
But lots of activity and
Coordination.

Rider: Very perceptive…You've got it.

And they'll *never* know?

Rider: Well, not really, except as we've spoken.
But there is one thing.

What's that?

Rider: The weather.

How so? (in unison)

Rider: We can't do this without
Interrupting weather patterns.

So this activity causes a storm,
Or storms, or what?

Rider: Just changes in weather.
It can't be helped.

(More riders thunder past)

Rider: Time for me to go.

Will you be coming back this way?

Rider: Yes, probably all of us.
This is a nice ride, very direct.

Good luck then, God's speed.

Rider: Thank you. Of course
You all realize it's not luck.

Yes. But do they?
Or will they?

Rider: They just…won't know.

Not a clue?

Rider: Just the weather.

Safe journey then.

Rider: Thank you all.

Stones
Winds
and Life

• 156

FALL THOUGHTS

The last leaves are holding on
Way beyond the others.
The winds come,
The rain,
They're still there,
Beautiful reds and golds,
Hanging on to the very end
Almost beyond their time.
Isn't Nature supposed to know?
Who are these stragglers,
These ones who mock the weather,
Who thumb their noses?
They're quite beautiful,
Resting at the ends of the bare limbs.
They stick out like little flags,
So pretty in the sun.

Maybe they're not listening.
They're certainly not giving up easily.
Hey! You've won.
You're the last.
You've proved your point.
Go to the ground,
Let winter in,
Let spring come.
Hey! Do you hear me?
You're holding up the process…

But they stay and stay.
Maybe they've nothing to prove.
No marathons,
No mountains to scale,
No armies to conquer.
Maybe they're just there —
Like the lingering tide,
Like the very last drop of snow to melt,
Like the last breath,
The very last breath.
Silently and peacefully they'll go,
A quiet parting from the branch
And a float to the ground.
Maybe as they dry
And blow along the ground,
Their noise will be heard —
The crackle of dry leaves
Blowing along pavement,
Startling at times if it's the only sound.

The last hoorah
For those sentries of color,
Nature's last banners.
Back to the soil.

But for now, they hang on.
Maybe they are the
Messengers of life,
A symbol of the whole,
Purely conceived,
Grown and nurtured,
Beautiful until the end,
Picking their time.

Stones
Winds
and Life

VICTORY

Each day the knights would
Go out with the army.
Each night they would come back.
Each time a little fewer.
Each time a little slower.
The carts would carry the wounded,
The air carried the moans and screams.
The jovial "Red" knight, as we called him, was gone first.
Then the "Blue" knight with yellow ribbons.
Then the "Green" knight.
Their ranks were thinning.

As children they wouldn't let us into the towers to see,
So we had to wait for the sounds.
The going was more upbeat, steady,
Some would be nervous, talkative,
Others to themselves — heavy, quiet, determined.
The bystanders reflected this mood.
Some would cheer,
Others were silent in prayer.
The younger more noisy,
The more experienced, quiet, resolute.

The clatter of hooves, the rustle of armor,
All followed by the wagons,
The "pickers" we called them.
Now they carried extra men.
On the way back they carried what was left,
Those who could be somehow salvaged.

It's rumored that we are winning.
Hmmm — so this is winning?
At first, each day younger men
Were recruited into the army.
Now older men are being recruited.
At first the knights were returning,
But one by one they are not.
Some just don't ever reappear.
There are still too many to count.
But it's the colors and horses to recognize
And try to remember.

Stones
Winds
and Life

It used to take a long time for the army to leave.
Now it's slightly quicker.
They march past in twos and threes;
It used to be in threes and fours.

Coming back has no tune,
No beat.
Words are muffled.
No one cheers at the drawbridge when they enter.
First the knights,
Then the horse soldiers,
Then the foot soldiers who can walk,
Then the wagons.

News? What's the news?
Have we won today, or lost?
Is victory near?
Are we holding them back?
How much longer?
Rumors fly as some dismount
And talk to relatives and friends.

Food is getting short
And the army must be fed.
Rationing.
Our stomachs hurt.
Events are slowing.
It is said we are losing
Fewer and fewer soldiers.

We are winning.
That is what they say.
Our relatives who can go to the towers and walls
Say that the enemy's fires at night
Can no longer be seen on the horizon.
The King now appears and even rides out
With the knights who are left.
Long live the King!
What a great victory!
Hooray for the King!
He has appeared and we have won!
The magic of His Highness has prevailed.

The knights on horseback were always
Tall and big.
The soldiers on horses or on foot
Were valiant as well.
It was the carts,
The living remains,
Level with our eyes,
Pieces you could touch,
Eyes staring back, not moving,
The sound of pain,
Appearing, then moving past.
They always came at the last,
Cart after cart,
Until we won.
Then there were only a few each time.
Then complete victory,
No more carts.

Back to normal.
The knights back to a regal look,
The King coming about,
Commerce picking up,
Produce and livestock arriving in carts.
Wood arriving in carts,
Across the drawbridge onto the cobblestones,
A familiar sound.
Victory! Freedom!
Life as before...

The sound of the cart
From the violence does not depart.
Through my soul it sends its chill.
I pray before I die it to be still.

LOST

My mind drops through the
Trapdoor of time and is
Suspended there.
I think I'll hang around.

The black sky reflects the sun.

The moonbeams meet the ice
And don't know where to go.

The volcano's lava hits the sea
And evaporates.

There are no dunes in the desert;
The sand floats above
The Earth as a sky.
Enter the void and visit
Times far apast.

Women are equal warriors.
They ride the steppes,
Robes and long hair flowing;
Decisive battles.

The crystal ball gazes into *your* mind.

Open the door and give the Earth warmth.

Pollution ends up in the toilets —
Some factories are overflowing,
Their executives must have
Large swimming pools.

Newspaper headlines:
    Love is Found
    Good Deed is Done
    Forgiveness Reigns!
    Touch Works
    Magic Child Heals Sick Parent
    Lawsuit is Dropped
        (All court participants
        enjoy feast and toasts)
    Neighbors Help the Elderly Rebuild
    Entire Town Gathers for Hugs

New *Good Glasses* actually reveal
People caught in an act of kindness.
    Feel good,
    Look good,
    Get yours today!
Sorry, all givxen out,
More tomorrow — Really!

           COME BACK ANYTIME
           We'll open up for you.

          ENTERING UNITED STATES
            INDIAN RESERVATION
       Please enjoy our abundant forest,
         lakes, and rivers. Thank you.

What dwells behind the mighty mask of power?
A tiny child stuffed in a closet of the parent's mind.

Listen, young child, life is simple.
To wit:
    One,
        I withhold my love until I approve of your actions, whatever they may be.

    Two,
        I can withdraw this love at any time without warning.

    Three,
        Don't question me, I'm the parent.

    Four,
        What was good for me will be good for you.

    Five,
        You can't go to bed until you finish your food.

    Six,
        This is a recording.
        Please rewind.

Stones
Winds
and Life

ABOUT THE AUTHOR

David Sweet, a lifetime resident of Tacoma, Washington, spends his time away from writing as an independent consultant specializing in self-actuation training for professionals, a real estate entrepreneur and as a grandfather. David enjoys the stimulation of working with his hands, restoring and remodeling.

Stones, Winds and Life has been a seven-year journey for David, one which evolved through his love of nature and the universe, and his belief they influence and are intertwined. He lives in Tacoma's north end with his wife Margaret, and is currently working on his second collection of poems and short stories.

NOTES:

NOTES:

NOTES:

NOTES: